YOU CAN COUNT ON YOUR "SIXTH SENSE"!

Do you ever wonder why some people seem to have exceptional luck . . . uncanny perception about people . . . consistent winnings on the stock market . . . unbelievable success finding lost items . . . "perfect timing" when asking for a raise or finding a great job? It's no accident. You too have intuitive potential waiting to be tapped. Professional medium Litany Burns shows you how to *transform your life* from the inside out. All her "secrets" are here, step-by-step techniques and exercises to teach you how to:

- Give psychic, psychometric and aura readings
- Practice clairvoyance and use it in your daily life
- Use telepathy and psychokinesis
- Release damaging stress
- Gain valuable insights often overlooked, hidden or ignored
- Cultivate healing inner harmony and share your newfound peace

LITANY BURNS, a professional medium, clairvoyant and healer for more than ten years, is an accredited teacher of psychic awareness in the New York State public school system. She has worked on the Son of Sam case and has also assisted corporations and medical personnel with her talents.

LOOK FOR LITANY BURNS'
DEVELOP YOUR CHILD'S PSYCHIC ABILITY
AVAILABLE FROM POCKET BOOKS

Books by Litany Burns

Develop Your Child's Psychic Abilities
Develop Your Psychic Abilities

Published by POCKET BOOKS

DEVELOP YOUR PSYCHIC ABILITIES

And Get Them to Work for You in Your Daily Life

LITANY BURNS

POCKET BOOKS

New York   London   Toronto   Sydney   Tokyo   Singapore

Illustrations by Janet Haber

Chapter-opening symbols are from *Symbols, Signs & Signets* by Ernst Lehner, Dover Publications, 1950

POCKET BOOKS, a division of Simon & Schuster Inc.
1230 Avenue of the Americas, New York, NY 10020

Published by arrangement with Prentice-Hall Press,
a division of Simon & Schuster Inc.

ISBN: 0-671-70138-X

First Pocket Books printing May 1987

10 9 8

POCKET and colophon are registered trademarks of Simon & Schuster Inc.

Printed in the U.S.A.

dedicated with loving appreciation
to
Frank Satir

Acknowledgments

I would like to mention the following people with appreciation for their help and encouragement in preparing this book: Karen Waldmann, Marilyn Beckford, Byron Nash, the Garsteins, Tim Sullivan, Dennis Fawcett, Jan Haber, Eloise Starkweather, and Althea Gustafson . . . with special gratitude and thanks to Joe Hazucha.

Contents

Contents

INTRODUCTION

The telephone rings. You answer it. The person you have been thinking about says hello.

You awaken from a dream. What you dreamed happens to you that afternoon.

Your dog is lost. Giving up your search, you make a wrong turn as you start for home and find your pet.

You walk into the wrong store in the shopping mall and find the shoes you have been wanting to buy.

You decide to take the long way home from work. Later, you hear there had been an accident along your usual route.

Someone comes to mind whom you haven't seen in years. Three days later you receive a letter from that person.

A fire siren sounds while you are sharing coffee with a neighbor. Alarmed, you rush home to find that you left the gas burner on.

You just lost your job. On the bus ride home you see an old friend who tells you of an available position in his office.

11

You are humming a song to yourself while driving your car. Switching on the radio, you find the same melody playing.

Coincidence? Luck? Mental power? Maybe. Psychic ability? Yes.

Haven't similar situations happened to you or to someone you know? And don't they keep happening? If you could understand how to use these abilities, you might be able to help yourself in your daily life situations. You might be able to benefit more from relationships. And you might be able to live a healthier, more productive life.

Everyone has psychic ability. Like any other natural talent, it needs only to be recognized and developed to be used. Some people can sit down at a piano and only attempt to play "Chopsticks." Give them a basketball or a knitting needle, computer or paintbrush and they will excel. Other people will be able to create beautiful sonatas and play them on the piano with little effort. Because psychic abilities are within us, they work in the same way. Some people will develop one of their abilities; some will develop only a few abilities, and others will be multi-talented. The chapters and exercises within this book will help you to discover which areas of your own psychic abilities you are most talented in and how to develop them for use in your everyday life.

There are no gimmicks, no years of disciplined training. Your psychic abilities are already there. They are as natural to you as your breathing. In fact, you use them everyday, usually without notice. You use them when you are relaxed and open, and then you forget about them—until you use them again.

Psychic ability—often referred to as Psi, ESP, intuition, or a sixth sense—is a way of perceiving and using energy that is different from physical energy to affect the physical world. Like any other talent, it does not desert you or diminish with age. In fact, it grows with you. You can develop it and use it whenever and however you wish. Like pitching a ball, dancing, writing, painting, singing, and being mechanically inclined, it needs only practice. The more you use it, the better it becomes.

If your psychic abilities have not been used since early childhood, they can still be developed fully. If you have been using them on occasion all during your life, you can still use them more. Developing them, whether at age two or eighty, depends solely upon your willingness to do so, because they are so interconnected with your very core of being.

Everything that is alive has psychic ability. Plants, animals, fish, insects—all possess their own psychic abilities. Many of these beings depend daily on their psychic abilities for their survival. They use them to protect themselves, find food and shelter, and adapt to their environment. As infants we are closest to our basic psychic abilities or instincts. Because our physical bodies are not yet developed, we rely on our sensing of things rather than thinking or feeling them. Like animals and plants we sense what will hurt us, what we need, and how to communicate those needs. As children, we spontaneously use our psychic abilities as natural extensions of ourselves. Many people have fond memories of imaginary playmates, seeing nonphysical colors and lights, and experiencing a greater sense of the simplicity of the world around them.

If you are curious about what these abilities are like on a very basic level, sit and watch a small child or an animal and they will show you. A cat might react strangely in the middle of a sunny afternoon by suddenly searching for a hiding place in the basement. Hours later a severe thunderstorm will occur. A small child may crawl into the lap of the crankiest uncle at the party and stay there, revealing the uncle's buried loving. A child may naturally take a crayon of a certain color and begin drawing a picture of an object she has never seen. A dog may sit by a door waiting patiently until his special friend comes home a day earlier than expected.

As we become adults we dismiss these talents. We learn to develop our intellect and emotions in place of them. Instead of using all of our faculties, we devise defenses that deny our initial and basic instincts and conform our trust to people and situations outside of ourselves. We grow so far away from our own inner voices that we become confused, angry, frustrated, and unhappy. How many times have you denied your own self and given in to the decisions and advice of others who knew less about your needs? Getting in touch with your psychic abilities is a way of returning to your early self without eliminating your emotions or intellect. It is a way to harmonize them so that you can make decisions and enjoy situations knowing you can trust yourself in anything that you do.

Much skepticism is associated with developing psychic abilities because they cannot be seen with the naked eye. Like any inherent talent—writing, composing, running, acting, painting—they can also produce physical, tangible results. So much information about the psychic world has been misconstrued or falsely depicted that we have come to recognize the entire range of possibilities through disastrous film adventures or sinister book plots. Used daily like any other talent, the results are sensational . . . to the people involved. Rather than hurt us, psychic abilities can provide meaningful insight, understanding, and knowing about ourselves and others that can be used throughout our lives to enlarge them. They are as natural and useful to us as laughter, creativity, and loving.

To develop these talents you only need to be willing to experience them. The rest is practice. By experiencing them in an open atmosphere you free yourself from preconceptions to explore the dimensions of yourself. Like flowers, they cannot grow and open without natural cultivation. Nature does not compete to be the best in its field. Each flower has its essence. This is also true of other living things, including people. There is no race or contest; no ability or amount of abilities is greater than another's. Each person has his or her own garden to cultivate; no more or less than needed. Once practiced, your abilities can grow and surprise and delight you like any other talent. The pleasure of practicing a piano to play a musical tune or knitting balls of yarn to produce a sweater is similar to the pleasure derived from developing and using your psychic skills. They add to your natural dimensions and help make you the special person you are.

Within this book you will discover words like *psychic reading*, *psychometry*, *auras*, *psychic healing*, *psychokinesis*, *telepathy*, and others, for abilities you are already using. You will discover new talents you never thought you had, and techniques to help you develop them. If you have little or no success in one area go on to the next. You may surprise yourself and with a little practice be able to accomplish what you could not do before. These abilities can work for you anytime and anywhere, throughout your entire life. Whether you are choosing the best cologne to wear, which business to merge with, how to kick the football between the goalposts or when to cash in your stocks, whether you can make the seven o'clock movie or send your child to the best camp . . . your psychic abilities will always be there to help you.

Put your misconceptions and restrictions aside. Your psychic abilities already exist. Allow yourself to be open and willing to explore them in your own way and time. You will learn about yourself . . . what you feel . . . what you can do . . . and who you are. They are your talents to enjoy and discover.

one

ENERGY

Where does this psychic energy come from? If we cannot see it, how do we know it exists? If we cannot measure it, how do we find its boundaries? If we cannot explain it, how do we trust it?

Psychic or nonphysical energy can easily be explained if you are willing to experience a different way of seeing things.

Imagine yourself greater than the borders of your body, for the moment, or ever greater than the room or place you occupy. Imagine yourself to be formless, like a cloud drifting in the sky. Allow that image to expand so your cloud surpasses the sky. That is what you seem like when you are psychic energy. Nonphysically you flow, like a cloud, changing shape and form.

Enlarge your energy or cloud until it fills a space greater than the world or universe. This is the sense of the non-physical energy of one person. Condensed to physical dimensions, your own energy may be large enough to fill the state of California or the entire Northern Hemisphere. The amount of energy you have is relevant to your growing. As each person learns and grows they add to this energy. It makes you no greater or less than any other person. This energy is simply what you are.

Because our bodies are physically separate, we tend to see our clouds apart from one another. Our nonphysical energies, similar to clouds, merge and flow together. Our clouds mingle like water rather than pieces of ice, each cloud adding its own nature to the whole. The size or form of each cloud is not important. It contains its own energy to share with and connect to all energy.

From your cloud, this nonphysical energy flows into your body through a channel directly connected to it. Some people liken this channel to an umbilical cord of energy. Your connection to this cord is located where your neck forms the base of your head. This connection is called your *energy exchange channel.* (See Figure 1.) Through this channel, our bodies release energy to and receive energy from our clouds for use throughout our lives. It is this energy that joins us to ourselves and to each other.

EXERCISE:
ENERGY EXCHANGE CHANNEL

To experience your own *energy exchange channel,* place your hand, palm open, upon the base of your head, where your neck joins, or hold your palm a short distance from it. Change hands from time to time if you wish. Relax and see what you experience. Some people may feel a tingling sensation or movement of energy in their fingertips or their hand(s). Others may sense, rather than feel, a current or flow of energy. Some may feel nothing at all. This is not a measure of your psychic ability or your psychic energy.

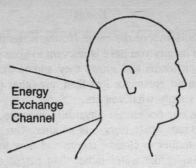

Energy
Exchange
Channel

Figure 1. Energy exchange channel.

It is only a way to acquaint you with a functioning part of yourself. Sense or feel the energy from your *energy exchange channel* during any part of your day. It is always feeding your body with energy that is you.

When your body is at rest, you experience this energy more fully. During sleep, your body does not need as much energy as it does when it is active. A minimal amount of energy always remains in your body to sustain its vital functions. The rest of your energy usually returns to its nonphysical state, your cloud, for that period of time. This process, called *astral projection,* occurs every night. You leave your body and return to your energy. We do this, sometimes more than once, during our sleep. It is a way of connecting more completely to our energy. When you are ready to awaken, your total energy returns to you once again to begin your day. Sometimes you are suddenly jarred awake for no apparent reason. You open your eyes, and your body feels as though it is shaking inside. This happens when your body awakens before all of your energy has naturally returned to your body. Because you need more of your energy to function consciously, the energy enters very quickly, causing a momentary imbalance of energy inside you. After a moment, your body resettles the energy, and you begin your day.

People experience *astral projection* at times other than while asleep. When undergoing surgical operations or traumatic life or death situations, you may leave your body and rejoin your energy to gain a better perspective of the situation or to gain more energy to help you during such events. When needed, the energy that had left, returns. Because you are attached to your energy umbilical cord, the energy never totally leaves you. With practice, one can *astral project* in a conscious state in order to gain insight and experience being on a nonphysical level.

Why do we leave our bodies every night? What do we do when we are away from our bodies? And how can we remember where we have been?

We leave our bodies for many reasons: to experience ourselves totally, to sense and communicate with others on a purely energy level, to connect with ourselves to gain a better perspective of our own energy and the energy we all share.

Away from our bodies and the physical world, we no longer adhere to physical dimensions such as time and space. As energy, we perceive the past, present, and future without time separation. Without physical boundaries we flow beyond speed perceiving possibilities of our future, changes from our past, and extensions of our present. Because we use our energy to grow and change at our own rate, our future can change as well. In physical nature, nothing is fixed and change is constant.

When we return to our bodies, we may remember where we have been. We may bring back a sense of other people or ourselves in that dimension. We may remember nothing of this experience, or we may, through our bodies, use our physical faculties to identify these experiences visually in thoughts, words, or images. Our bodies serve as physical translators of this energy and our experiences of it. When we awaken, we can learn from these visually translated images. Such images or thoughts are called dreams.

DREAMS

Not all dreams are prophetic memories of *astral projection*, but all dreams work with our energy. Some dreams are a way for the body to release images accumulated daily. The images and thoughts are released by the brain and converted back into energy dispersed by the body. Impressions from such dreams may be retained or forgotten. Some dreams are simply a way for the mind to rid itself of excesses so it is not overloaded.

When such images or thoughts are clearly retained by the body or repeated in various ways, they usually have relevance to a situation or problem you are consciously facing. For example, you may have a dream or series of dreams consisting of many symbols, or people, or situations resembling short movie scenes. When you awaken, one scene, or person, or situation remains clearly in your mind, and you feel a reaction to it. Usually such a scene or situation, accompanied by your reaction, remains to give you insight you may not have readily gained while conscious. In its resting state, your body is removed from external distractions and can work on its own problems and solutions. This homework is carried over into a waking state when the situation is important to your growth.

When our dreams focus on events yet to happen and are vivid, they are more psychic in nature. When dreaming or upon awakening there is, at first, no emotional reaction to them. They are simple informative perceptions, brought back with you from your nonphysical energy for physical use. The emotional reaction(s) occur after we think about the information, adding to it our own physical feelings or fears. If, for example, you dream of a fire in your friend's house, it does not mean you are creating the fire or that the fire itself will ever happen. It is something you have remembered from your dream. If the image is strong and enduring, tell your friend about the dream. He or she may inspect the wiring and find a faulty connection and prevent the actuality of a fire. Instead of burning flames, a volatile argument which could have serious repercussions for your friend, may unexpectedly have taken place with a member of the family. Your dream may help initiate insight and understanding to prevent such a heated situation. Rather than harbor doom and destruction, these dreams can facilitate learning and growth.

Precognitive dreams, ones in which you receive information regarding future possibilities, can also help prepare you for natural daily situations: a possible meeting with a new friend, an encounter with an old foe, or a job cancellation for example. We are not always aware of our *precognitive dreams.* When a physical situation or event occurs that has previously been experienced in our dreams or nonphysical travels, it feels overly familiar to us, as if we have lived it before. Such experiences are called *déjà vu;* those already seen, but not momentarily remembered. With insight and dream experience, we can use these instances to gain a better understanding of ourselves.

One way to begin to know your psychic abilities is through dreams. For many people it is an easy way to allow any form of information through without subjecting it to mental expectations, preconceived notions, or fears. In its resting state, your body is less apt to block the energy and information that come to you for utilization in your waking state. As you become more comfortable with this process you will be able to receive such insight and information in a more clear and concise manner.

Exercise: Dreams

If you would like to remember your dream to gain added insight and knowledge, there are several things you can do. Take a piece of paper (or a pad) and pencil and place them in an easily accessible space beside your bed. Before retiring for the evening, ask your body to help you remember your dreams upon awakening. As soon as you awaken, write your remembrances on the paper beside you. Date your writing and keep it in a log with others. This way you can refer to it from time to time to observe connections or recurring patterns or themes shared by various dreams. As you practice this exercise, you will find that information pertaining to your daily life will be easier to recognize and that you will be able to remember more and more of your dreams. If some of your dreams are precognitive in nature, you may want to reread them at a later date to see how they relate to your life since the time of your dream.

As you become more comfortable with this process, you will be able to have your body wake you during the night to write down impressions exactly when they happen. With practice you will also be able to have your body help you to retain only the information related to your learning and to release from your memory excess information already worked through.

For additional resources, you may read through the many books on the market that interpret symbols and images derived from dreams. To benefit most fully from your dreams and your dream experiences, use these books as references when you do not comprehend instances in your dream(s). You will find that if you allow your own facilities to work with you, you will, with patience, by the process of rereading your written dreams, be able to interrupt your dreams in a more personalized manner. If you become confused about the dreams you are having, ask your body, before sleeping, to help you clarify them by allowing through other information. Your dreams will continue to aid you in your growing on an energy level, or in a more conscious waking state.

Our bodies are sustained at all times by this energy, even when we *astral project*. When your physical life is over, all energy within the body returns to its nonphysical energy or cloud, leaving the body behind.

What does it feel like to be this energy? Is it different from the way we feel inside our bodies?

Outside your body your energy is not restricted. Bodies are constructed to meet physical needs and to function in a physical environment. If you were without your body, you would not walk, you would flow. Without your physical abilities, you would not speak or think, you would sense. You would not be physically separate from others but would merge and flow with all energy.

The closest sensation we have as physical beings to this energy occurs when we are infants. Without developed brains, emotions, and verbal capabilities we sense and react to our environment on a basic minimal level much in the same way as animals and plants do.

Exercise: Feeling vs. Sensing

To experience the difference between physical and non-physical perceptions on a simple level, this exercise can be used: Take an orange, pencil, or small object, and hold it in your open hand. Place your hand, palm upward with the object inside it, away from you. Close your eyes. Without using your fingers or other parts of your body, sense the object. Sense its dimensions, its essence, and the energy inside its physical form.

Open your eyes and, using your vision and fingers and hand, feel and see the object. Explore the object using your other physical senses such as taste and smell. Try this experiment with several objects individually until you experience a difference in perceptions.

If you wish to sense your environment, situate yourself in a park, house, room or other natural setting. Close your eyes and sense what is around you separately and then all together.

Open your eyes and using only your physical senses, mind, and emotions, observe the same situation. Practice this in the same setting or in different settings to perceive the differences between your physical and nonphysical abilities.

Walk through your day sensing and then feeling people as you encounter them. You will find through experience that when you sense people you are not restricted by their physical condition, size, shape, sex, or color. Nonphysical energy does not differentiate by physical standards. It is energy that we all use and share.

Our energy is our main source of life and the development of our creative and psychic talents. It enables us to add to ourselves and harmonize with every other person regardless of physical distance or cultural difference. Through our bodies we use and share this energy from our nonphysical source, whatever you believe it to be, to grow dimensionally. We each embrace it as a vital part of our lives.

Questions and Answers

What does a recurring dream mean?

A recurring dream can be a situation or thought that the body has a hard time releasing and is constantly replaying when at rest. Insight can be gained by remembering and working with the information so the body can release it. Before sleeping, ask your body to draw more energy so you might gain more insight within your dream about the specific situation if you do not understand its meaning.

On a psychic level, a recurring dream may relate events to come or a memory from your past that will help you with a current situation or problem. Within the dream there may be a message from a loved one or an old memory that, once recognized and not feared, can be released and used as an aid in your growing process.

If we all derive from the same energy, why don't we all look alike?

Basically we are alike. Our bodies are constructed the same internally and contain the same processes. Since we all grow at different rates and experience different learnings, our bodies are individually adapted for our own growing. A person may be more endowed with physical dexterity and power because he is learning about himself through sports activities or mechanical capabilities. Another person may be handicapped culturally or physically in order to learn more about his internal strength. Ways of learning are relevant to the individual involved. You may learn different things in society by having a female, rather than a male, body. Our essentials are the same and we add to ourselves through our unique individual learnings. These learnings benefit not only ourselves but all living things who share this energy.

Can our energies be dangerous to us in any way?

No. Your energy is a natural part of you. It is the life force that sustains and enhances you. Since it is such an integral part of you, it can only complement you. If you choose to close yourself off from the potential and capabilities this energy provides, you can inhibit yourself and cause confusion and frustration in your daily life. This energy is no more dangerous to you than your own body and life.

What does it mean when I dream about a dead relative? And why would I dream about him at a certain age rather than the age when he died?

There are many reasons for a dream of this nature. Psychologically, you may be working through your physical emotions about the person or about the loss of that person. Psychically, you may have communicated with him while *astral projecting,* when both your energies were most connected. Since your body interprets such a meeting in a way physically comfortable for you, you may visualize your relative at a time when you were most compatible or when you were most aware of your connection to him. This way, the memory of the meeting on an energy level would be more physically accessible to you upon awakening.

Is this energy finite?

Many people relate this energy to a source such as God, a religious figure, universal consciousness, or love. Whatever source you feel comfortable with is valid. This energy, as mirrored in our physical environment, is always changing and developing. With physical matter, nothing is ever destroyed; nonphysically, energy is always evolving, shared by all and used as a loving source for learning.

Are animals and plants more developed than humans because they are closer to their energy?

Animals and plants are not closer to their energy. They have a different learning that does not involve the cooperative use of mental and emotional abilities on the same level as humans. We all share this energy and use it for our growing on whatever level we can. People sometimes confuse their basic sense of themselves and their energy by over-utilizing or underdeveloping their own complex physical learning capabilities.

two

PRELIMINARIES

Since our psychic abilities are natural, we can use them to help us in our everyday activities; yet many people fear change, their future or even their own potential. How can you trust that what you cannot see, and sometimes do not even recognize, will help you? What happens when you get so nervous or distracted that you lose your sense of what you are actually feeling? How can you use your psychic abilities when you are in situations that could change your life? Usually such situations call for concrete answers and split-second timing. What happens when you have no verifiable information on which to depend, except a feeling? How can you trust this energy?

GUT RESPONSE

Your gut or solar plexus is where all of your nonphysical and body energies combine. It is the one point in your body

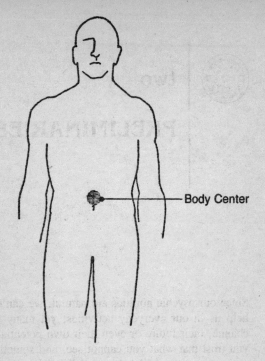

Body Center

Figure 2. Body center.

that is central to you. It is your crossroad of energy. This place, located near your stomach, is called your *body center*. It is the focal point for your psychic energy and is where your reactions and feelings will be the strongest. (See Figure 2.)

Your gut is like a light inside you. It fires your desires, leads you to move, and draws you to others. It is the connector for you to all things that are good and right. If you focus away from your light, you will not clearly sense the heart of the matter before you. You will rely on other lights for solutions or live in the darkness of your fears and anxieties.

We focus on all types of physical distractions: the job, other people's defenses or feelings about us, the remark made, the money. Without a basic sense of yourself within the situation, none of these externals can offer the most reasonable conclusion for you.

Your light is very simple. It always shines no matter how dark the tunnel you have dug for yourself. It shines toward the best path for you. By following your light you will be able to lead yourself from pitfalls, avoid dead ends and roads filled with obstacles.

If your light is not known, you rely on others whose ideas and perceptions are removed from you or even on your own heightened emotions which can add unwarranted fears and imaginings. Without using your gut you move farther and farther away from yourself and your own natural talents, compensating for them with defenses that inhibit you and cause you pain within a situation.

Your gut reaction at your *body center* simply reacts to everything you do. If what you are doing is conducive to your energies, it reacts positively in a simple visceral manner. If you are doing something against your basic self, its visceral reaction is negative. There are no explanations or psychological reasons involved. The reaction is a simple physical feeling of yes or no. It is like a loyal friend or conscience that never leaves you no matter how much you ignore it. It reacts to every decision you make, large or small, important or immaterial. It is the willingness to use it that enables you to remain productive and harmonious within yourself.

Many people disregard their gut feelings and rely on their defenses. For example: you have made plans with your friends to go out to dinner. All week you have been looking forward to this. Then one of your friends calls you and cancels. Instead of contacting the other people involved to maintain the date, which is what you want to do, you defer to your friend's wishes and reschedule the dinner for the following week. "It's all right," you say, "I don't mind," or "It really wasn't that important."

Even when your friend suggests that you call the other people to keep the date, you defer. What you have done in this instance and probably in many others like it, is to go against your initial *gut response*. You have gone against the flow of your body and nonphysical energy. In doing so, you have gone against yourself.

Some would say, that in this particular situation, it was not important. The dinner itself was not as important as the way in which you reinforced your actions to negate yourself. You stopped relying on yourself, causing you to distance you from yourself; a step that, in order to gain from your living, you must, at some point, retrace.

Many people have strong *gut responses* and ignore them. They add excess psychological, theoretical baggage to their initial visceral response. Over a period of time they may even develop chronic psychosomatic histories of insomnia, indigestion, intestinal disorders, headaches, bowel problems, and other physical ailments. The stress accumulated when going against yourself can drain or overstimulate you.

How many times have you felt that you knew what to do in a given situation and yet accepted someone else's solution because you felt unsure, afraid, defensive, or confused. By listening to your simple visceral responses, you could have avoided needless pain, apprehension, worry, self doubt, and fear.

How physical is a *gut response?* And how will I know it? What if I have gone so much against it that I will not find it? How can I really trust it?

Your *gut response* is your most practiced psychic ability. Used since birth, it is the basis upon which you instinctively sense right from wrong. The more you recognize your gut response, the more you can work consciously with it. For some people it is a physical sensation in the pit of the stomach. For others it is a faint nagging inside. For many it has come to be known as a source of pain, for it actually feels like a leadened weight or illness inside you as you continue to go against yourself over and over again. Since, no matter what you do, it is your first response to any decision or action, you can come to recognize it at any time during your day.

Exercise: Gut Response

A basic way to accustom yourself to your *gut response* is to ask yourself a simple yes or no question that involves little emotional involvement: whether you should have that cup of coffee, which outfit to wear to the party, what movie you want to see. Make a concrete, yes or no decision, and see what you feel in your solar plexus. You will have a visceral response to your initial decision. It will be distinct and simple, never conflictive or confused. Practice this several times until you have a good working sense of your *gut response*.

If your gut is your initial response to a situation or question, your mind is then the body part used to devise meaning and action for your decision. Your gut is your barometer; your mind your activator.

Exercise: Gut Response vs. Mind Action

Ask yourself a question concerning a problem you are having. Focus on the problem and, using your mind, think about the problem, worry it, exhaust all possibilities of action for a solution, both pro and con.

Clear your mind and ask the question again allowing only your gut to physically respond, yes or no.

Take the same question and find your *gut response* again.

Now using your mind, based on your *gut response,* think about the problem and its solution. You should experience a difference in your evaluation of the problem.

If you find yourself answering the question with "But if I choose this . . ." or "If I don't do this . . ." when you are seeking your *gut response,* you are compensating for it with thoughts from your mind. Clear your mind and start again or get busy doing something physical that will distract your mind like sorting papers or washing dishes. Then ask the question again.

If you are undecided or find no response at all, ask yourself another question or return to the same question at a later time. You may be trying too hard to find your gut reaction or you may be overlooking it. You will get the same response each time you ask.

Your *gut response* will always prove its worth to you. To experiment on a higher level, use your gut to make every decision for the next week and use your mental abilities to follow through with these decisions. Whether you decide which brand of cereal to buy, whom to invite to the concert, what to say to your partner or spouse about a mutual situation, or when to wash the car. Let your basic psychic ability and mental capabilities work together to help you. You will always feel your *gut response* first and your thoughts will then add to your initial response.

You will find that over a period of time your *gut responses* will work with you, helping you to become who you are. By trusting yourself, you will, with little effort, build confidence and a sense of balance and self worth that will help you in overcoming restrictive fears and defenses.

By practicing your *gut responses* with simple decisions, you will find yourself better able to pull away from emotions and defenses that blind you when having to make decisions of major importance.

When you begin to use your other psychic abilities in

more focused ways, your gut will help you sort through impressions and information coming to you. These impressions, like your *gut response,* will not usually fit into your own psychological thought process. Before you think, the information will pop into your mind. It may come in the form of an idea, disassociated words, feelings, or thoughts. The information may not flow in sequence from one thought, word, or sentence, but may come in spurts, separate from one another. Rather than confusing you or mixing with your own thoughts, your *gut response* can serve as an indicator about each impression received. It will help you to know what information you can trust and what you may have manufactured. It will help clarify impressions and verify them for your use.

Your *gut response* will also help you to become independent in your own thought process, discarding thoughts that are irrelevant to the situation. Even when you solicit friendly advice, you can use your *gut response* to weigh information given so you can use only what is valid for you.

Ask yourself the same question over and over again and you will receive the most valid response. Even if you are in a situation that changes, simply ask your gut about the situation as it now exists and you will receive an appropriate response. As you change and grow your *gut response* grows with you. It is immediate and simple and always there.

If trusting your *gut response* enables you to rely on yourself in situations, what happens when other people are involved in the same situations? Will your *gut response* be right for them as well?

If you are right for you, you will be right for the entire situation in which you are involved. If you go against your own true feelings to accommodate the needs or desires of another person, how will you be honest to yourself and to them? If you are doing what is best for yourself based on your *gut response*, you are also allowing the other person to discover what is right for him. By refusing to reinforce his defenses or wishes in a false manner, you permit him an atmosphere in which to decide freely what is best. An atmosphere of this kind promotes honesty and sharing rather than sacrifice and resentment. You have afforded that person a chance to see the games he may be playing with himself, thus denying his own happiness. You have no right to demand his honesty, you only have the opportunity to be honest with yourself. If you are being true to your own core of energy you can extend your energies to be shared in a loving and respectful way with others because you are responding from a place inside yourself that you can believe in.

For all the times when you said, "I should have listened to myself," "Why did I follow him?", "That's what I originally felt," or "I knew it!", you now know what you haven't been doing: trusting your *gut response*. You never have to conjure it up. It is always ready and willing to respond.

RELEASING EXCESSIVE ENERGY

You are driving your car to an important job interview or taking a crucial exam or meeting your in-laws for the first time or getting psychic impressions.

When situations arise that are important, we tend to worry, analyze our every move, and rehash doubts and insecurities. The energy created by this stress flows through our bodies and adds to existing anxiety, nervousness, depression, and may even create physical body pain.

An easy way to relieve yourself of this excessive energy is to drain it out of you. The release of this energy does not eliminate your basic amount of energy. It eliminates the extra energy that disrupts your own energy balance and flow.

Exercise: Releasing Excess Energy

Clear your mind of all thoughts so you do not perpetuate these negative feelings which add excessive energy. Think of something calming, something pleasant to you. Place your feet solidly on the floor, ground, or floor board of your car, wherever you happen to be.

Place your hands onto an inanimate object, anything that is not living: a desk, the sides of your chair, the kitchen sink, steering wheel of your car, your shopping cart, and allow the energy to drain from your body out through your hands and feet.

Be careful not to place your hands or feet upon your own body or the body of another person, animal, or plant. The energy you are releasing will not harm them but it will disturb their natural balance of energy just as it disturbed yours. Any inanimate object is the best recipient for this energy, which will dissipate and not be recycled. Allow the energy to continue to flow out of you until you feel more calm and peaceful or until you sense that you want to take your hands off the object. When you feel balanced again, you can resume your regular activities.

You may feel the energy drain from you. You may feel nothing at all. This is not a measure of your psychic ability or your lack of perception of yourself. It is an exercise you can practice daily to relieve yourself of needless tensions.

If you feel you have not released enough energy, remove your hands, shake them vigorously and replace them onto the inanimate object. The more you practice this exercise, the more you will be able to sense when you have accumulated extra energy and when to rid yourself of it.

You can also *release excess energy* every evening before you go to sleep to ensure a more peaceful, rested sleep. Place your feet squarely on the mattress and your hands on the side of the bed or on the mattress itself. Allow your body to drain any excessive energy it may have accumulated during the day. Whatever energies remain that still cause you imbalance may be those that you perpetuate within yourself. The more you work with your *gut response* and use your mind as a working mechanism of your body, the better you will be able to determine what you do to throw yourself off balance.

Releasing energy can be done in the presence of others without their knowledge. Sit at the lunch table and ask for your promotion with your fingers holding the menu, your feet resting comfortably on the floor. Talk to your child or friend while driving your car and *release excess energy* into the steering wheel. Sit at your desk and listen to test instructions while you *release excess energy* into the sides of your chair. Answer your prospective mother-in-law's questions while you rest your hands beside you on the sofa cushion. No one will notice and you will feel more able to handle the situation.

RELAXATION

Trying too hard for results stops your natural flow. If you are not calm and relaxed physically, you can close yourself off to perceptions and information that may help you.

Relaxation is an important factor when maximizing your own abilities. How many times have you forgotten an important point in conversation, a name, or word, or number when you needed it, and tried to recall it? Usually, after much frustration, you give up trying and allow your mind to freely move on to another thought. It is then that the name or number or word comes floating back into your mind. Because you have relaxed enough to allow your mind to focus, the information can be received readily.

Since everyone has psychic abilities, there is no need to push for results. In fact, by pushing you block with your own tension whatever impressions come to you. If you concentrate, you overwork your focus. If you relax your mind, you allow yourself to focus naturally upon the information you are receiving. Developing your psychic abilities is not like cramming for an exam. It is a life-long exercise that can be practiced daily in a calm and easy manner.

When you begin to practice your abilities it is a good idea to use all of the *preliminaries* mentioned in this chapter before attempting any exercise. They will help you to be less restrictive in your focus and enable you to read your impressions more clearly.

Exercise: Total Relaxation

Situate your body in a comfortable position wherever you are: in a room, outdoors, standing in line at the checkout counter, or waiting in the dentist's office. Make sure that no part of your body is physically restricted. Clear your mind of all thoughts for the moment.

If possible, close your eyes and focus on your physical body. Beginning with your feet, feel your toes and relax them. Feel your feet and relax them. Move on to your ankles and relax them. Continue feeling and relaxing each part of your body: your calves, knees, thighs, pelvis, inner organs, lower back, stomach, upper back, chest, shoulders, arms, hands, fingers, neck, head, face, ears, eyes, forehead, until you are totally relaxed. If you feel a part of your body tensing again, go back to it, feel it, and relax it.

Stay relaxed and experience your entire body. Relax yourself into your gut and center yourself in your *body center*. Travel to any part of your body and feel it in its relaxed state. Your body is a whole being. It is your house where you physically live. It protects you and nurtures your energy on a physical level. It is where you breathe and learn. Focus on your breathing. This is your own natural rhythm. It is here where you use your psychic energy. Each time you feel yourself tensing or losing focus, relax your body and feel it again.

Total relaxation is something you do with yourself for yourself. Use it before you begin a psychic exercise or when you want to feel open and calm to experience yourself in any situation.

COLLECTING ENERGY

The last step in the *preliminaries* is *collecting energy*. It is a way of consciously connecting your body energy to the energy of your cloud or nonphysical self to give you total focus on whatever you are planning to do. When you *collect your energy* to practice your psychic abilities you gather your resources inside and outside your body to use them more fully when receiving information.

Exercise: Collecting Energy

Release excess energy, practice *total relaxation*, and locate your *body center* or gut.

Clear your mind of all thoughts and focus on your cloud, drawing it to you so that its positive energy fills and surrounds you. Sense your nonphysical energy and commune with it just as you would do if you were praying, opening yourself to its beauty. Then focus on the activity you want to try.

Collecting energy is a way of pulling your resources together for focus. When you concentrate on this energy you limit yourself. Concentration is a body exercise using the mind. Focusing allows you to open to the potential of your energy, expanding your scope from your body to include your entire self. Once you have a clear sense of yourself and feel focused you are ready to begin any exercise.

Use any and all of the *preliminaries* for any activity that calls for focus. Whether you are facing an important board of directors meeting, competing in a sports event, playing a musical instrument, performing a play, or making an important phone call. These steps can be used any time and anywhere to prepare you for important life situations. When using them with your psychic abilities, practice them often: *gut response, releasing energy, relaxation,* and *collecting energy,* so they will always be available to help you utilize your energies. By themselves or in conjunction with your psychic abilities they will enable you to enjoy and be more aware of yourself in everything you do.

Questions and Answers

What if my friend and I both feel right about a decision, but I don't feel it in my gut. Is it still right for both of us?

If you go inside yourself for a moment, and ask yourself the question again, you will feel an immediate *gut response.* Whatever your response is, that is your answer. We are so used to making quick decisions based on momentary convenience rather than self awareness, or deferring to an authority figure who knows little about how we live inside, that we absently agree for the sake of agreement. If your *gut response* conflicts with your friend's decision, follow it and see where it leads you. Let your friend find his or her own *gut response* to make sure that neither of you is going against himself. If both responses are yes, then you have made a decision that will benefit you both. Situations change as the people in them do, so check your *gut response* throughout the situation to benefit fully.

Is my gut response *my emotions?*

Your *gut response* is your most basic emotion, because it is derived from loving yourself and being one with your energy. As we grow away from ourselves, our emotions become based on insecurities, other people's reactions, and fears. At times your emotions may become so entwined with past memories of feelings that your gut may conflict with your present emotional state. When you listen to your *gut response* and trust it, you are returning to the best foundation for your other emotions to be built upon.

Can my gut get angry with me and refuse to respond if I continually ignore it?

Your *gut response* is a part of you and not a separate being that dwells inside of you. It is your internal compass, pointing you in the best direction. It always responds. When you are angry with yourself and refuse to heed its response, it will not lessen, but will always be there for you anytime you are willing to sense it. It is you who might not respond to your gut feelings, not the opposite.

What if I am releasing excess energy *and I get interrupted? Will the energy have to be released all over again?*

You can stop releasing energy whenever you want. If you are interrupted, simply begin again. The energy, once released, is no longer inside you and will not return. The remaining excess energy can be released into an inanimate object when you are ready.

What do I do if I've drained excess energy, start to use my psychic abilities, and I become overwhelmed or nervous?

Relax. You may not have allowed yourself to release all of the excess energy inside you or you may not have relaxed or collected your energies before beginning your psychic exercise. *Release excess energy* again until you feel calm, then use the rest of the *preliminaries* before beginning. Repeat this process several times until you feel less nervous and calm.

What happens if I forget to release excess energy?

Your psychic abilities will still work for you, but you might find yourself a little more tense or nervous than otherwise. At any time, before using your psychic abilities, while using them, or after using them *release excess energy* if you feel confused, anxious, nervous or unfocused.

Can I substitute a yoga exercise for total relaxation?

If yoga exercises help you to relax and allow you to feel comfortable with yourself, then use them. Use whatever exercise is best for you along with *releasing excess energy* and *collecting energy*. A combination of yoga exercises may be helpful as long as you do not need specific amounts of space or time to perform them.

Can I meditate before beginning any psychic exercise?

If you are used to meditating for relaxation and focus, add your meditation exercise to the *preliminaries* in place of *total relaxation*. If you feel meditation will help you with *collecting energy* for focus, then use it in conjunction with the other *preliminaries*. Meditation can increase your sense of your body and/or your energy when used knowledgeably. If you are not used to meditation or if you have problems meditating, then use only the *preliminaries* before you begin any psychic exercise. Remember that there might be instances when you will want to use your psychic abilities for making split-second decisions or gaining quick daily impressions when time is not available in quantity. In such instances, unless you are quite practiced with meditation, you might want to use the *preliminaries* to facilitate your psychic process.

What if I need to use my psychic abilities on the spot and don't have time to relax myself totally?

Do the best you can. Once you practice all of the *preliminaries* together before attempting each psychic exercise, you will find they will become automatic and take up very little of your time. Each *preliminary* will be natural to you and can be accomplished with little preparation.

Can I use my psychic abilities without collecting energy?

You can use your psychic abilities every day without actively *collecting* your *energy*. You will find that when you do *collect* your *energy* in a conscious way, you will achieve more focus and produce clear and tangible results with less interference.

If I have certain difficulties is there something else I can do? Should I be persistent?

Usually by persisting you concentrate more and close yourself off from your perceptions. This creates expectations, tension, and frustration. If you need to visualize your cloud, a deity you are comfortable with, or a sense of yourself when *collecting energy*, then do so. If being verbal when *collecting energy* is helpful in the beginning, then speak your thoughts. If you wish to stay in your gut or *body center* to gain a sense of yourself, you will find it will help to give you balance when *collecting energy*. It will give you a physical focus since all of your energy centers there.

Can I draw too much energy?

You will draw as much energy as you need and as you allow yourself to use. You are not actually drawing more energy inside yourself, you are focusing yourself on the energy already inside and around you in order to perceive it more clearly. If for any reason you find your body tensing or reacting to the energy around you, just *release excess energy* and continue. The energy is not harmful because it is your energy which you are using.

three

PSYCHIC READING

Everyone has given a *psychic reading* on a minimal level at some point during their lives. Some may call it "a feeling about something that has no reason," "a good vibration from someone," or "a lucky hunch."

Psychic reading is the ability to receive vibrations of energy from another person, place, or living thing and translate it into words or thoughts. When you use this ability in a focused way you are, in fact, acting like a human radio; fine-tuning yourself to this energy and transmitting it verbally.

You naturally sense each person or situation with which you come in contact before you think about them. When you give a *psychic reading,* you take this sensing of energy a step further. By verbalizing impressions received, you are able to communicate to the person you are reading information about themselves without your own preconceived notions or thoughts. It is a way of giving objective insight without the interference of your own mind or emotions.

Psychic reading is not mind reading. What you are reading goes beyond the person's physical characteristics or reactions. You are reading their energy and not their momentary thoughts. Psychic energy, unlike mental energy, is not confined to the physical moment, but encompasses elements of the person's past, present, or future. Fortune telling is a common term for *psychic reading*. When telling a fortune, your focus is relegated more toward future possibilities than past or present situations.

Psychic reading, used for yourself, can help you gain valuable insight often overlooked, hidden, or ignored. When reading for another person, you can relate insight and impressions about the person that might have taken months or years for them to recognize and use. By verbalizing the impressions received you make available to people a wide range of information about themselves: their early childhood experiences that might have bearing on their present problems, a future possibility for a job change, a new way of dealing with a recurring problem, or a latent talent they have yet to experience fully.

A *psychic reading* is not a power directed toward another person. It is an honest and objective way of communicating information. You will find that as you read for people they will assume responsibility for working with or ignoring insights gained. Because this ability is natural, like all of your other psychic abilities, the more you practice the more you will benefit.

With each *psychic reading* you will learn more about yourself, even when you are reading for others. You will notice how you restrict yourself and your own potential, and how you perpetuate certain defenses, insecurities, and blocks in other areas of your life. By practicing *psychic reading* you will become more adept at distancing yourself from your own personal thoughts, prejudices, or emotions, thus allowing your psychic impressions clarity.

Be patient with yourself. *Psychic reading* is not a contest nor is it a measure of your own self worth. There is no success or failure when giving a *psychic reading;* there is only learning. Let your psychic abilities prove their tangible worth to you. If you were an artist, just discovering your talent, you would need time and practice to experience what you are capable of achieving. You would not expect yourself to paint your finest masterpiece in one sitting. Your psychic talents will develop at your own rate. The more you work with yourself, the more developed they will become and the more readily available they will be at any moment during your daily life.

When you first translate psychic vibrations into words you will find that each word does not come into your mind in exactly the same way. Rather than your previous hit or miss instances, you will experience moments when no information is forthcoming or moments when information is coming very rapidly and filling your mind with thoughts and perceptions. The process will be very erratic at first. When you unclog a drain in a sink that hasn't been used regularly, the water does not at first run smoothly through it. Like a physical sink, your body is also unclogging your nonphysical drain, which hasn't been used regularly. There will be blockage and overflow of information entering your mind from time to time. As you practice *psychic reading* you will clear your drain and find that the flow of information will run smoothly whenever you focus on this energy.

Your own thought process will be different from the way you receive psychic information. Rather than in logical sequence, you may at first, experience impressions about the past, present or future mixing together without time differences. As you allow more information to enter your mind, the information will help serve to differentiate itself and to form its own time sequences.

By using your *gut response* along with all the information received, you will be able to clarify the difference between your own thoughts or opinions and the information you are reading. Simply ask yourself if the impression is your own thought and your *gut response* will answer you, yes or no. The more you use your *gut response* within your *psychic reading*, or any *reading* you are giving, the more it will respond readily to the information as you receive it without having to stop for clarification. You will learn to sort through information and fine tune your human radio to sense impressions and apply them to the person or situation you are *reading*.

There are several reference guidelines for beginning a *psychic reading* or any *reading* using your psychic abilities. As you practice your own techniques and abilities these points of information can be of added benefit to facilitate the process of the *reading*.

DO'S AND DON'TS WHEN READING

1. Practice preliminaries before attempting any reading. The *preliminary* exercises will help you keep your mind and body relaxed and focused on the activity you are practicing. The flow of information will be less blocked or interfered with when being received.

2. Verbalize any and all information coming into your mind at the time of the *reading*. Do not try to control impressions you are receiving. Words or images, numbers or thoughts which have no immediate purpose, may come to you at any time during the course of the *reading*. As you verbalize your impressions you will find that succeeding information may clarify previous impressions. Your *gut response* also will help you interpret your own response to information coming to you. You will find that the person you are reading for will be able to piece together the words or thoughts in their own logical sequence since the information is being given to them for their benefit, not yours. They will naturally be able to apply the information where needed. You do not create the information, you read their energy. Like a radio, you are the receiver, they are the transmitter.

3. Do not push for information. When you start your car, you turn the key in the ignition, press your foot on the accelerator, and put the car in gear before you move it. By using the *preliminaries,* clearing your mind of your own thoughts or ideas, and feeling focused and relaxed you will bring your psychic abilities into constant use. If you race to capture the impressions, your mind will become filled with your own thoughts and preconceptions. Your feelings will begin to override the natural flow of impressions, and your psychic abilities will stall out. This does not mean they will not start up again. By allowing rather than competing, focusing rather than concentrating, receiving rather than expecting results, you will again be able to receive and communicate impressions.

4. A *reading* does not have to be future oriented. You may receive, within the course of a *psychic reading* or any other *reading* involving your abilities, impressions relating to the person's relationships, their personality strengths or weaknesses as applied to a situation, or their unused talents, ways in which they stop themselves from enjoyment or insight into past and present situations that immediately affect their behavior. The purpose of any *reading* is to focus on the person being read at that time rather than the type of information coming to you. Each *reading* will be different, based on the information pertinent to that person.

The practice of verbalizing impressions, accompanied by your *gut response* as your barometer, is your main goal.

5. Do not fabricate information to fit the person's needs. *Psychic reading* is not a personality contest or a means for seeking approval from another person. The main goal of any *reading* is to gain insight and information to be used for growth and learning. You are not reading a person to impress them. You are relaying information they can use to see things about themselves they would not readily see. Your own personal wishes or hopes or defenses have no place in a *psychic reading*. Your simple yes or no *gut response* will help tell you when you are invading the information with your own thoughts or feelings. Even if you start to add bits and pieces of your own insights to the *reading*, your *gut response* will react to them, helping to alert you to what you are doing. If, at any time during the *reading*, you are unsure about the information you are receiving, verbalize it. Your *gut response* will respond viscerally to help you to separate yourself from the information given. When this happens, stop for a moment, clear your mind and relax. Then allow the impressions to continue.

6. Some information will be more clear in your mind than other information. As you verbalize information some words or thoughts will provoke a stronger *gut response*. This will tell you that information is important to the person you are reading. They may, upon hearing it, choose to disregard it or even negate the information given. Trust your *gut response* and continue with the *reading*, telling the person each time you react strongly to the information. Your intention is to receive the information as clearly as possible, not convince the other person to use it.

If you receive two opposing impressions at the same time, verbalize each of them. As you do this, your gut will respond, helping to clarify the information given. When you are giving a *reading* you may jump from one time frame to another without consistency or thoroughness. Allow the entire *reading* to be given without trying to discover what is most important to the person. Your *gut response*, along with the full impressions verbalized, will help the rational mind of the other person to sort through the material and put it in logical working sequence for him.

7. If the information comes too quickly or confuses you do not stop the entire *reading*. If you are feeling overwhelmed by the information you are receiving or are blocking impressions, sit back for a moment, and repeat the *preliminaries*. Sometimes we place too much value on our own performance in front of people rather than on trying to experience and discover our techniques and abilities during a *reading*. If you are interfering with information because you are afraid to appear foolish or be wrong, take a moment to look at those fears. For no other reason, the *reading* you are giving will be of added benefit because you will be able to discover and possibly work through a problem that might inhibit future *readings* you give. If you are encountering such fears or defenses when giving a *psychic reading*, you are probably letting the same fears stop you from realizing your potential in other areas of your life as well. The more you learn about yourself through giving *psychic readings* or other *readings* that use your nonphysical abilities, the better you will be able to resume your growing in a fruitful way.

8. Do not edit the information you are receiving. Whatever impressions enter your mind, communicate them verbally as best you can. You have no right to decide what is or is not important to the person you are reading. By editing information you put yourself in a judgmental position, allowing your own thoughts, ideas, defenses or prejudices to replace the information you are receiving. What may seem difficult or negative to you is not always the same for the other person. What you might choose to edit could be of great importance to the well-being of the other person.

When people begin to give *readings* to others, they are afraid they are going to receive information about a death. If, during the *reading,* that information is coming to you, you have no right to delete it. In those limited cases, when this does happen, the person being read is usually aware of the situation beforehand. The *reading* is not a harbinger of bad news but a reinforcement of the person's own perceptions which can allow him to accept what he already knows. What you may be reading as a death may not actually be a physical death in some instances. You may be relating the death of an old pattern of living that has been a hindrance to the person and would be well discarded. By editing the information at any point while it is coming to you, you may misinterpret the essence of the information, and leave the person or yourself with a lingering feeling of dread, guilt, or confusion. In certain instances, a person forewarned of the death of a loved one, will have the insight and opportunity to clarify misunderstandings and share themselves with that loved one before they depart. You are not deciding life or death situations for anyone, you are reading the person's energy as it is projected to you.

9. If a person asks a specific question and there is no information coming to you, do not stop the *reading.* Relax, and see what other information comes to you about that person. If you are blocking information, your *gut response* will help you get out of the way. If you feel clear and the information is still not being received, ask your gut whether you are supposed to give the information concerning the question. If the answer is yes, practice *preliminaries* and continue with the *reading*. The answer to the question may surface within the information being given. If your *gut response* is negative, it may mean that the person is supposed to find the answer to the question through his or her own experience. Rather than coming from a second party, the learning will be better received through first-hand experience. You may not receive the fact that it is their learning; you may just not get an answer to their question. Communicate your responses as you receive them and let the other person decide what is the best solution.

10. Be fair to yourself. You are a human being with your own physical limits. Everyone wants to know more about themselves. People will, when involved with information about themselves, forget about the person who is giving the *reading*. It is your responsibility to establish time periods when it is convenient for you to give *psychic readings*. If you want to give a *reading* to a friend, allow yourself a time when you will feel relaxed and not distracted by other daily responsibilities. Having to take the roast out of the oven or expecting an important phone call during the time of the *reading* will only interfere with your focus.

If you do not receive concrete information in a clear manner at first when you attempt a *reading*, do not give up. This does not mean you are incapable of giving a *reading* or that you have no psychic abilities. It probably means that you are expecting too much from yourself and are closing yourself off from the information coming to you. Only you can stop yourself from developing or challenging yourself to discover more of your talents.

11. You can be wrong when giving a *psychic reading*. Giving wrong information during a *reading* does not make you invalid as a *reader*. It does not even make the *reading* you are giving entirely wrong. You may be confusing information you are receiving when you verbalize it, or picking up vibrations from another person sitting near the person you are reading. You may be conveying past information with present insight or in a present situation. If information given at any point during the *reading* is off target or wrong, do not make excuses. Go on with the *reading*. If you stop yourself and become involved with your own insecurities or poor self-image based on the information of the moment, you may never allow yourself to experience the rest of the impressions coming to you. Relying on your feelings of uncertainty may prevent continuation of the *reading* and the realization that you also can be right.

12. You should be able to receive impressions any time, anywhere, for any person. Certainly trying to read for someone in the middle of rush-hour traffic has its limitations. Aside from avoidance of physical disturbances, you need no proper surroundings or setting in which to give a *psychic reading* or any other *reading* using your psychic ability. There is no special time in which to give a *reading* except a time when you feel comfortable and relaxed. There is no special bond you have to have with another person to read them effectively. You do not even have to like the person you are reading. Your personal feelings are not involved when the information begins to come to you. Since you read people and situations in a minimal way very naturally throughout your day, do not devise specific stipulations for your *readings*. Practice giving *psychic* and other *readings* in different settings to many types of people at various times of the day and year. This will prevent development of unnecessary blocks that might inhibit your use of your abilities.

Give a *psychic reading* for an infant or an old man, a

new business or spring flower, a pet dog or new boss. All can be read easily if you are willing. If you find yourself physically tired or emotionally drained by your own problems at the time of a *reading,* reschedule it for a time when you will be more focused and relaxed. With practice you will be able to incorporate the *preliminaries* so that even during those times of fatigue or stress you will be able to read adequately. Your psychic talents are as portable and as adaptable as you are.

13. Do not ask for any information about the person before giving the *reading.* The less information you are told about a person, the more chance you have not to involve your own thoughts or perceptions within the information received. When you first begin to read another person you might feel uncomfortable not knowing anything about them. Think back to the times in your life when you had certain hunches or insights about a person or things that came to pass. In each of these instances you had little or no information to use, just the clarity of your perceptions.

If you do get stuck at the beginning of a *psychic reading* or other *reading* using your psychic abilities and find yourself having a hard time allowing the information into your mind, relax. There is no race to begin. *Collect your energy* for focus and begin again. If you still receive no information, and you can't seem to find out how you are blocking yourself, have the person you are reading ask you a specific question or give you a certain area to focus on, like their job, their family, or their special friend. Do not have them tell you about themselves or circumstances concerning their question. Simply have them ask a question. The problem is that your focus is diffused, not that you are unable to read them at all. By having a simple question on which to focus, you can allow the energy to flow and the impressions to come into your mind.

When giving a *reading* to a friend or person who you know intimately, it is helpful to begin with a question asked to enable you to pull your own feelings and expectations away from the information received. Use your *gut response* as a barometer to keep your emotions in check and not let them distort the information you are giving. With practice you will find less need for questions asked at the beginning of a *reading* as you naturally remove yourself from the information you are receiving.

These pointers are not steadfast rules. They are guides to help you develop and explore your own *reading* techniques more freely by minimizing problems you may encounter from time to time. If you approach each *reading* as a developing exercise you will find your abilities flourishing and becoming more easily accessible to you.

GIVING A PSYCHIC READING

How do you give a *psychic reading* to yourself? How do you give a *psychic reading* to another person? Are the *readings* very different?

Since you are most involved emotionally with yourself, it is sometimes harder to remove your own feelings from the information you are receiving during a *psychic reading*. By trusting your *gut response* through the entire *psychic reading* you will be able to allow more energy to be interpreted and utilized for your own growing.

When giving a *psychic reading* to another person you will find that you use the same process but have the added benefit of distance from the emotions and feelings of the other person you are *reading*. The restrictions you place on yourself when facing another person are your own and are not, in any way, derived from the other person.

Exercise: Giving Yourself a Psychic Reading

Situate your body in a comfortable position, standing or seated. Allow yourself minimal distractions during the time of the *psychic reading*. There should be no phone calls nor interference from physical obstructions; no photographs nor writing on the walls around you; no other people present.

Release excess energy into the sides of your chair or any inanimate object.

Relax your body totally and center yourself in your *body center* to feel your *gut response*.

When you are relaxed, *collect* your *energy* in order to focus on the exercise you are about to begin.

Clear your mind of all thoughts or impressions and sense your body. Close your eyes, if you prefer, or allow your vision to rest on a blank wall nearby.

Allow a word or thought to come into your mind. (If you wish to record your impressions, place a tape recorder near you before beginning and switch it on as the words come to mind. Leave it on for the duration of the *psychic reading*.)

Speak any and all words, thoughts, sentences, or impressions that come into your mind. Do not think about them, but allow yourself to repeat them. When the thought or word is finished and your mind is blank, clear your mind again and allow another word or thought inside it.

Continue verbalizing, stopping only to clear your mind or repeat *preliminaries* when needed.

When there is no more information entering your mind, sit back, replay the information on the recorder or remember it in your mind. Do not evaluate it, just listen to it.

If you feel inhibited using the tape recorder or verbalizing out loud, write your impressions down on a piece of paper as they come to you and then read them at the end of the *psychic reading*. If writing down words distracts you from relaxing and focusing, then simply verbalize them to yourself. You may find that by standing before a mirror, you will be able to distance yourself from your thoughts and use your reflection as a focal point for the *reading*. You will find the best means of communicating the information the more you practice.

Some of the impressions may be confusing at first because you are opening up your nonphysical drain and learning how to use your mind and body to help you. The more you acquaint yourself with the process of *psychic reading*, the more impressions you will be able to receive.

Since you are subject to your own blocks when giving a *psychic reading* to yourself, you may find that you will facilitate your own psychic process by having a specific question to focus on that has little emotional involvement. By asking a question of less emotional importance you reduce your chances of interfering with the information coming into your mind. As you practice, you will begin to sense your own physical reactions to the psychic information you are receiving. Your *gut response*, when in doubt, will serve as a viable barometer.

If you find yourself unable to perceive personal information for yourself, you might want to try giving another person a *psychic reading* before reading for yourself. The fewer demands you place on yourself and the information, the more readily you will begin to experience your abilities.

Exercise: Giving a Psychic Reading to Another Person

Situate your body in a comfortable position near the other person you wish to read. Any place or position is acceptable, as long as you are in physical proximity to the other person. Allow enough light in the room or space between you so that you have a visual sense of the person. This will allow your body to be more comfortable with the person.

When giving a *psychic reading* to someone other than yourself it is best, at first, to be alone with the person so that the energies of other people do not interfere with the *reading*.

If you would rather write down your impressions than verbalize them directly to the person, have a piece of paper and pencil close to you. As you practice reading, try to verbalize as much information as you can without writing it down. This will allow you to become used to your talent in a natural way without relying on specific tools outside yourself.

Explain to the person you are reading what you will be doing so they too will feel comfortable. If you wish, have them practice *total relaxation* with you to ensure a conducive atmosphere for the *reading*.

Whether they join you or not, *release excess energy*, *relax* yourself *totally*, sense your *body center*, and *collect* your *energy*, focus on giving a *psychic reading* to the person before you.

Clear your mind of all thoughts. Then look at the person's eyes and allow the words to come into your mind. By focusing physically on their eyes you create a visual connection to their energy, the eyes being the "windows of their soul." If you feel uncomfortable or if doing so distracts both of you, settle your eyes on a part of their body (a shoulder, for example). This will give you a physical contact for focus. If you find yourself not wanting to look at the person in any way, either close your eyes or focus on a blank part of the wall near the person.

If you find, during the *reading*, that you want to combine

any of these focal points or keep your eyes closed throughout the *reading,* do not stop yourself. By practicing and exploring ways of reading, you will find the best way for you to connect yourself physically to their energy.

Take a deep breath, and with your mind cleared, allow whatever thoughts or words that come into your mind to be spoken. Verbalize them as soon as they come to you. Do not wait for your voice to work separately from your body or for the other person to respond. *Reading* is a natural process. You will speak as you normally do. The only difference will be that you are not thinking about the information as you might in having conversation. The thought or word will pop into your mind without thinking. As soon as it appears, whether it be a feeling, a color, a situation, sentence, or series of sentences, verbalize the information as best you can. Your *gut response* will help you keep your own feelings or reactions from entering the *reading.*

Relax and continue verbalizing impressions as they come into your mind. Do not push, simply clear your mind after each impression and wait for the next one to arrive. Pause to *release energy* or to focus again when necessary. You are not being judged by how fast you can give the information nor even how capable you are. The person you are reading is probably more focused on his own thoughts and reactions to the information than he is on you or your performance during the *reading.*

If, at first, you feel more comfortable writing down your impressions, make sure all impressions are written before sharing them with the other person. Allow all information concerning a thought or impression to be written before going on to the next impression received. Writing down every word or thought may, however, inhibit your flow of information. Therefore, whenever possible practice verbalizing any and all information.

The *psychic reading* is concluded when no more information is entering your mind or when you feel you have finished reading. If you are in doubt about ending a *psychic reading,* relax, clear your mind, and see if additional information is present in your mind. Ask your *gut response* if the *reading* is over. If your response is negative, practice *preliminaries* and see what other information comes to you. If your response is affirmative, tell the person you are reading that you are finished.

There is no set length of time for a *psychic reading.* If you wish to continue to receive impressions after the *reading* is over, have the person ask you specific questions. This will enable you to focus on receiving more information, if desired. Any additional questions should be asked at the end of the *psychic reading* unless, at some point during the *reading,* you are unable to receive information readily. Questions can interfere with the free flow of information and should only be used to augment or enhance the *psychic reading* itself.

When you first attempt to give a *psychic reading* to another person there are a few ideas to keep in mind about your choice of subjects:

1. Work with a person who is willing to let you explore your abilities without interruption or restriction. A person who is open to what you are doing and willing to give you honest feedback about the information rather than your performance will enable you to experience your talent in a supportive atmosphere.

2. Do not try to read for a person who is closed or hostile to what you are doing. When you are beginning to relate to your own abilities you are not meant to be tested or judged. Learn to appreciate your ability without the added burden of pressure or performance.

3. If you are reading for a close friend, treat the information the same as you would when reading for anyone else. The information is totally independent from what you feel and should be allowed to prove itself. For example, if you receive impressions about a divorce for your friend, you are relating information about a possibility in his life. You are not deciding their fate or even giving your opinion about the situation. The information you have given is ultimately his to work with or ignore. Your responsibility when giving any *reading* is to be open and honest about the information you are receiving about the person. If, before you read for a friend, you explain the nature of the process for receiving psychic information, you will be able to avoid any preconceived notions and both of you will benefit from the *reading*.

When you begin to give *psychic readings*, think of yourself as an explorer. The more you open yourself to the information you are receiving the more you will discover about yourself and your psychic abilities. Like lifting the layers of a curtain, what is not obvious initially will become more and more vivid as you continue. Proceed at your own rate of discovery and experiment with your own techniques. If you are caring and considerate of yourself and your own abilities, the people you read for will reciprocate.

Exercise: Group Psychic Readings

If there is more than one person interested in giving a *psychic reading* or if you wish to feel the support of a group when beginning to read, this simple exercise can be used.

One person, picked by the group, should be situated in front of the group, the others placing themselves in a semi-circle around him or her. The person in the center of the group is the subject to be read. All others will be *psychic readers* for the duration of this *reading*. When the *reading* is completed, another person from the group can be chosen to be read by the group. This can be continued until all persons have had a chance to be read by *psychic readers*.

Each *psychic reader* seated in the semicircle should have full visibility of the person being read. Their bodies should be in comfortable positions and paper and pencil should be in front or beside them.

All *psychic readers* should follow *preliminaries: Release excess energy* into the chair or floor beside them, practice *total relaxation*, and *collect* their *energies* to focus on the exercise of reading the person before them. Each person should follow the preliminaries at his or her own pace, clearing the mind and feeling a *gut response* when ready to begin.

As each *reader* feels calm and focused, each should allow his vision to focus on the person's eyes, a section of the person's body, or a place on the wall or area nearest the person being read. Each person will have his own way of physically connecting with the person being read. There is no competition involved. Each person should begin when ready and proceed with the *reading* until he feels it is finished.

As words or impressions come to mind, each *reader* should write them down on the paper before him. Clear the mind after each impression and allow all other impressions to follow. All information should be written down until no more impressions are forthcoming.

When finished with the *reading*, each *psychic reader* can place down the pencil and wait for the rest of the group to finish. While waiting, if another impression comes to mind, write it down. Do not alter or analyze or rewrite any impressions already written.

When all have completed their *psychic readings*, take turns sharing each impression out loud among the group.

If each wishes to keep his impressions anonymous, have the person who is the subject of the *readings,* collect the papers and read aloud the impressions to the group, while commenting on the accuracy of each *reading.*

This exercise can be used and continued until the group concludes the exercise. Be sure that each subject being read contributes to the verification of information received.

DAILY USES FOR PSYCHIC READING

Your *psychic reading* ability need not be used for anyone else but you. It is your own option whether or not to give a *psychic reading* to another person. Your *psychic reading* ability can be for personal use in any activity of your daily life.

If you are a parent trying to teach and understand your child or children, a teacher planning a curriculum for the members of your class, an occupational or physical therapist giving attention to your patient's needs, a boss seeking to take maximum advantage of the talent his or her workers, use your *psychic reading* ability to gain insight into the other person(s) with whom you are dealing.

If you are a brother or sister trying to get along with your sibling(s), entering a relationship, or continuing to nurture a long standing relationship or marriage, use your *psychic reading* ability to help you understand yourself and the other person in the situations you experience together.

If you are a lawyer defending your client in court, read the judge and the prosecuting attorney to gain added benefit when building your case. If you are a therapist creating a conducive atmosphere for growth for your client or a nurse attending to the patient's or doctor's needs in finding the right treatment, let your *psychic reading* ability help you.

If you are a policeman interrogating a suspicious person,

a business person assessing the needs of your client, an agent dealing with career decisions or a car mechanic hiring an extra worker, use your *psychic reading* ability to aid you in your decisions.

In any situation or occupation when dealing with another person you can read the person before taking action. Whether you are asking for a raise, a loan, a favor, seeking a favorite restaurant, or deciding which cashier at the grocery store will be the fastest with your order, your *psychic reading* ability will help you.

If you want to start out on the right foot in your new job or enhance your relationship with your boss or co-workers on your current one, use your *psychic reading* ability. Read your prospective in-laws before you marry into the family, or your child when he is crying. Go to the pet store and read all the puppies before choosing the right one for you.

You can use your *psychic reading* ability to help those closest to you when they are in trouble or lost inside themselves. You can help yourself when you have an argument with someone you love by psychically reading them. It will enable you to pull your own defenses and emotions away for the moment and face the problem as it really is.

Each time you are offered a service or buy a product from someone, read them to determine the validity of the product they are selling you, whether they be an insurance person, a mechanic, a real estate person, a gardener, or a baby sitter.

As a student, professor, athlete, artist, professional or nonprofessional person, you can use your *psychic reading* ability to help you develop a productive atmosphere in which to work and grow. You will see yourself and your environment more clearly and enter into situations or make associations that are of benefit to you.

As in life, everything changes as people and situations change. Your *psychic readings* and information will change accordingly. A person you may have read a week ago may change and so will the information you will receive about him. Each *psychic reading* is as unique as the person you are reading, including yourself. They are the transmitters, you are the antenna.

Although this talent is fascinating and helpful, you have no right to read anyone who does not wish to be read in a formal *psychic reading.* If a close friend is involved in a situation that affects you, read them in relation to yourself in the matter. Each person has his own right to his way of growing. *Psychic reading* is not a power you can use to dominate other people; it is a learning tool to be shared.

You will find that even if you wish to use your *psychic reading* ability to persuade other people to change their behavior, you have no control over their use of the information you have given. It is their right to decide what is best for them. Accepting or rejecting the information given is not a measure of your love for them or their love for you. Let the results of your *reading* stand by itself to be proven with time and change.

Experiment with your *psychic readings.* If you receive tangible results through giving information, enjoy them. If you do not receive results immediately, do not give up. Try again and work on the blocks in yourself that prevent the information from flowing. The more you read, the more understanding you will gain about yourself and the more trusting and confident you will feel about your own abilities. Nothing is rigid. Practice and develop your own techniques to allow insights to flow freely. Keep reading, nothing can stop you except yourself.

Questions and Answers

Will my abilities stop working after a while if I continue to use my psychic readings *to impress people?*

Your *psychic reading* ability will continue to work with you at all times. You might find that if you continue to give *psychic readings* to impress people, your ego and emotions might interfere with the information and taint your impressions. Your *psychic readings* will work best when you are able to free yourself from false images of yourself. As you continue to read for others, you will find your *gut response* will help you to become more at ease with yourself, allowing the proof of the given information to help you feel confident and more worthy. You will be able to see yourself and develop your loving and psychic abilities in a more honest and enduring way than you had before and naturally eliminate a need to impress others.

What do I do if a person reacts to the information I am verbalizing in a psychic reading *and leaves the room?*

Do what you feel comfortable doing. Ask your *gut response* to validate whether or not you have given the information honestly and openly to the person. The person may have left because you touched certain defenses to which they reacted, and they may not want to change at this time. They may have had expectations for the *reading* which you could not fulfill even at your best. If you feel you have interfered with the information, you may want to speak with the person and explain what has happened, giving them the option to have another *reading* at a later date. The *psychic reading* is not a measure of your worth or your psychic talents. It is a learning tool. With each *psychic reading* given, you will learn how not to repeat mistakes and how to open yourself to receive the full benefit of the *reading*.

Will it help me to touch the person I am reading during a psychic reading?

Psychic reading does not need any physical contact from

the other person. Their physical presence is your contact enabling you to receive their vibrations and translate them into words.

How can I read information for myself more clearly when I am facing an emotional problem or I feel blocked?

This is often difficult because when you are reading yourself you are both the transmitter and the antenna. At such times, when information is needed, it is sometimes best to distract yourself with physical activities after doing the *preliminaries* for focus. This will enable you to keep your mind free from your problems, at the moment, and focused on a meaningless physical act. You may have to repeat this several times before the information can come through. Your *gut response* will be a great help in separating your own thoughts or fears from the information you are able to receive. Try to keep yourself as calm and centered as possible during the time of receiving information.

Can you set a time limit for a psychic *reading?*

After giving several *psychic readings* over a period of time, you will have a rough idea about the time needed for your *readings*. Always allow yourself extra time with the person you are *reading* to enable you to receive all information coming into your mind. Each *psychic reading* will be different, but a general estimate of time spent for a *reading* based on experience will help you set specific limits.

Can a psychic reading *be given over a long distance, for example, over the telephone?*

As long as there is some physical contact with the person, their body seated beside you or their voice communicating over the telephone, a person can be read psychically. If a person is physically present their energy will be clearer to you, but in the case of an emergency or a factor of distance, a *psychic reading* can be given satisfactorily in this way.

Is there a limit to the number of people in a group psychic reading?

There is only a limit to the number of people involved in a *group psychic reading* when time is a factor. There should be enough time for each *psychic reader* to be able to receive and communicate all information to be given. An additional number of people in any *group psychic reading* can give added reinforcement of information already given, or produce more information for the person being read.

Is a group psychic reading *better than a regular* psychic reading?

A *group psychic reading* can aid in giving reinforcement to information and add new insights, as stated above. However, the addition of people can also cause possible confusion when you are beginning if you are unable to focus clearly on the subject being read or are distracted by the movements of the other *readers*. A *psychic reading* sometimes involves very personal information which the subject might not wish to share in a group situation. The choice of *psychic reading* situation should be made by the person being read.

four

PSYCHOMETRY

As a psychic talent, *psychometry* is the next best thing to being there. It is the ability to read people by looking at their photographs or by holding a possession of theirs without having the person present during the *reading*. During a *psychometry reading,* the photograph or the object serves as a physical contact for you to the energy of that person.

A *psychometry reading* is similar to a *psychic reading* because you are reading the energy transmitted by the other person and translating it into words. The main difference between the two is that in a *psychic reading* the person is always present, even if you are reading them over the telephone. In a *psychometry reading,* you are reading the person's energy through a physical representation of him; either a photograph or object(s) without the person actually being present.

For some people, giving a *psychometry reading* is easier than giving a *psychic reading* because there is no other person present to watch or listen to you. For others, a *psy-*

chometry reading is too removed from the person and there is no opportunity for immediate reaction to the information given. For those who are comfortable using both these psychic talents, a *psychometry reading* can be incorporated within a *psychic reading*. When people you are reading wish to have more information concerning their relationships with other people not present during the *reading* they can hand the *reader* a photograph or object relating to the other person involved and be able to receive viable information about that person in relation to themselves. The reading of the objects or photographs of other people is not a violation of their privacy, but is a way for the person receiving the *reading* to gain insight and understanding into the personal situations that involve them.

PHOTOGRAPHS

A photograph of a person is a reproduction of the person. When the photograph is taken the whole person, including his or her energy, is present. A *psychometrist*, one who gives *psychometry readings*, can then look at or hold the photograph and be able to read the energy of the person in order to give information and insights. This nonphysical energy has no physical boundaries and can project to the *psychometrist* information concerning the person's past, present, and future.

Since the *psychometrist* is reading the energy from the person and not the physical characteristics of the person, it does not matter whether the photograph is black and white or color, or whether the photograph was recently taken. The photograph itself only serves as a connector to the person's energy. It does not even matter whether or not the person lives nearby or is deceased. His energy or cloud remains with him.

Many people involved with primitive religions refuse to have their photograph taken, because they feel that their cloud or soul will be captured on the film and this will remove some of their spiritual powers. *Psychometrists* have come to know, through practice, that the essence of a person can only be represented, but cannot be captured on film. A painting or drawing of the person can also be used in a *psychometry reading*, but there is the interference of the artist's own energy to contend with. When an artist paints a picture of a person that is true to life, the artist has, through the activity of painting, added his or her own energy to the canvas and the paint simply by touching them for a period of time.

When beginning to read using *psychometry*, it is best to avoid complicated situations such as paintings. Any photograph can be used as long as the person you are planning to read is clearly in focus and view. An unclear representation or partially obscured form might confuse and interfere with a beginner *psychometrist*. It is also better to start with a photograph of the person alone. Other people in the photograph may distract you just as other people present during a *psychic reading* may confuse the information being received. If you cannot find a photograph to read which shows only one person, then use a photograph in which the person is clearly defined, with the other people in the background, or in which the person is depicted with just one other person. The more you practice your *psychometry* talents, the easier it will be for you to read any photograph showing your subject in any situation, alone or with a large group of people.

Exercise: Psychometry Reading with a Photograph

Situate your body in a comfortable position in a place where you will not be distracted. Place in front of you the pho-

tograph of the person you wish to read. Try to use a photograph of a person about whom someone has full
knowledge so that you can speak to them after the *reading*
to gain feedback about your impressions. It will be of little
benefit to read a photograph about which no one has previous knowledge. The feedback will enable you to gain
more confidence about the validity of the information received. If, in the course of the *reading,* some of the information is not verifiable, you may want to talk to the person
you have read to see if they can verify it.

Practice all *preliminaries: release excess energy, total
relaxation, collecting energy.* Locate your *body center* and
sense your *gut response.* If you need to repeat some or all
of these steps during the *reading,* do not hesitate to do so.
Any and all of these steps will help you to focus and relax
when needed.

When you feel ready, hold the photograph in your
hand(s) or lay it face up so you can see it clearly.

Remove all thoughts from your mind and look at the
eyes of the person in the photograph. You may want to
cover the person's face below the eyes for better focus.
You may also want to look at the person's entire face or
body for focus, or you may decide to look at the photograph and then look away from it, from time to time, allowing your eyes to rest on a blank wall or space in the
room. Explore a wide range of techniques to find the one
most suitable for you.

Some people feel they become too concerned with the
physical characteristics of the photograph and lose the focus of the person being *read.* Others find that, by having
a visual contact, they can receive the information more
consistently. As you practice, you may find a variety of
techniques that will be valuable to you within the *psychometry reading.*

As you look at the photograph or look away from it,

allow all thoughts, words, colors, or sensing to be verbalized as they enter your mind. Repeat these impressions as soon as they come to you, much in the same manner as when giving a *psychic reading*. Do not stop the information or delete any impressions. The less you program the way in which you receive information the more information you will receive. Your *gut response* will serve as validation for all impressions coming to you and will help to keep your own feelings from intruding upon the *reading*.

If you feel more comfortable writing down your impressions, have a piece of paper and pencil nearby. Since we usually speak faster than we write, it may be easier to verbalize your impressions to the person who brought the photograph to you or into a tape recorder to replay them later for verification.

Allow the information to continue, stopping when you feel confused or when no more information is forthcoming. Relax, clear your mind and try again to see if more information comes to you to clarify a point or to add to the *reading*. When all information has been received, or when you wish to stop the *psychometry reading*, place the picture down and allow any excess energy to be drained through your extremities.

Try reading several photographs, at different times, of various people in diverse settings. Do not let physical limitations such as age, gender, background, size, or eyeglasses, stand in your way. Your goal is to read the energy of the person as openly as possible. Try reading a photograph of an infant or a pet to add to your reading experience. As you practice, you will find that background or even your own familiarity with the person you are reading will not interfere with the information coming to you.

If during the *reading* you feel blocked, stifled, confused, or distracted, relax, practice the *preliminaries*, clear your mind and start again. If you begin to feel tired or frustrated, do something else for a while and return to the *psychometry reading* when you are ready. There is no deadline for un- folding your abilities, they are always with you and ready to be used.

Exercise: Group Psychometry Reading with a Photograph

To experience your psychometric ability in a group setting, three or more people should participate.

Assemble several people as when giving a *group psychic reading*. Choose one person to sit in front of the group and hold the photograph. All other members can sit or stand comfortably in a semicircle around the person, making sure that each person will be able to see the photograph once the exercise has begun. The people in the semicircle will be the *psychometrists* and should have paper and pencil beside them.

Before the photograph is displayed, each person, includ- ing the central person, should practice *preliminaries* and locate his *body center*.

When everyone is ready, the photograph may be held at a comfortable position for all to see. All *psychometrists'* minds should be clear and open to receive any and all impressions coming to them. As information is received, any words, or thoughts, should be written down. Continue writing impressions until your mind is clear again. If you become confused or distracted, use your *gut response* to help clarify information for you, clear your mind, relax, and begin again. When all information received has been written down, place your pencil down to signify you are through with the *reading*.

After every *reader* is finished, share the information un- til all *psychometrists* have had a turn verbalizing their impressions. It is most important to have at least one person present who knows the subject you are reading to help verify and clarify information received. If this is not possible, schedule a time when the person in the photograph or someone knowledgeable about him can be available to meet with the group to give positive feedback about impressions.

If you have several photographs available, each member of the group, in turn, can hold a photograph before the group so that each member can experience using *psychometry* and receiving valuable information about someone they know.

OBJECTS

When using an object during a *psychometry reading* you are also reading the energy of the person. The object itself, having been worn, used or touched by the body, retains some of the person's energy within it. If the object has been used consistently by the person over a period of time, the object will retain a clearer imprint of the person's energy.

There are times when you are given a piece of jewelry, a dress, a coat, or an heirloom from a relative and you have a strange sensation upon wearing it, as though the giver is there with you. They, of course, are not physically present, but if the object was worn or loved by the person, his energy vibrations can remain. Again, this energy is not taken from the person involved. It is a projection of the energy. Just as a tape recording of your voice does not take your voice away from you, a projection of his energy does not diminish his own natural balance of energy.

An added benefit to a *psychometrist* when reading an object is that the object itself may retain a history of energy stored inside it. For example, when reading your great grandmother's wedding ring, which has been handed down successively to the women in her family, you may also be able to read the history of all the people who have worn it. *Psychometry* is a valuable way of giving personal histories, or of dating art objects or archeological artifacts when no information is known.

There is no one type of object that is easier to read than others. Certainly an object that has little or no contact with a person would be difficult to read. An object that has passed through many hands may create confusion but, with practice, could be read by a *psychometrist*. If the energies of the people involved are not distinct, the item has not remained with them for a long period of time or is not used frequently, the energies within the object may be harder to read clearly. In such cases, impressions of the person who wore or used the object most often would be read more clearly than those who had only limited contact with the object.

An object, like a photograph, can also generate information about a person who lives far away or who is deceased. An object last touched centuries ago can be read as clearly as an object held by someone in the present, since psychic energy is not bound to the convention of time.

Exercise: Psychometry Reading of an Object

Have the owner of the object enclose it in an unmarked, untouched envelope. This ensures that the object has not been touched or held by someone other than the owner. The added benefit of a sealed envelope will free you from being distracted by any of the object's significant and obvious physical characteristics when giving the *reading*. For example, if you are reading a man's wedding ring, you will be able to avoid your own physical assumptions that might interfere with the free flow of information. With practice you will be able to hold an object, without covering it, and read its energy.

The person presenting you with the enclosed object should not disclose any information about the object or its owner. Let the object rest in its envelope before you. Do not touch or feel the object to determine by its size and shape any preconceived ideas about it. Have the person who has given you the object verify all information after the *psychometry reading* has concluded. If the person is not available at the time of the *reading*, ask them about your impressions at a later date.

Release excess energy, practice *total relaxation*, and locate your *body center*. *Collect* your *energy*, allowing yourself to focus on the object you wish to read.

Clear your mind and touch or lift the object into your hand(s). Without using your tactile senses, relax your fingers and allow any information to come into your mind. Verbalize all impressions. If you want to place the object down before you and touch it from time to time or change hands while giving the *reading*, do so. You may want to place the object in your lap, touch it to your cheek or forehead, or simply place one finger on it. The object is a contact with the energy of the person who owned it. Experiment with several techniques until you find the best way for you to receive clear information.

If you reach a stopping point in the *reading*, place the object down, practice *preliminaries* if needed, and begin again. Continue reading until all information received has been verbalized. If you choose to write down your impressions, remember the process of touching and using your hands to hold the object in this exercise will be interrupted. It is best to verbalize when possible. If you feel a need to write down your impressions, hold the object, place it down and write your impressions, then hold the object once again to gain more information.

When the *reading* is concluded, you may open the envelope to see the object and gain verification. You may also continue the *reading* after having opened the envelope, by holding the object in your hand and verbalizing additional impressions received.

If the object you are reading is too large to be placed in an envelope, hold the article in your hand(s) or station yourself near it so you can touch it from time to time to connect yourself to the energy inside it. Verbalize all impressions that come into your mind for the duration of the *reading*.

Exercise: Group Psychometry Reading of an Object

Rather than using several objects, if more than two people are interested in developing their psychometric abilities, this simple exercise can be created.

Take a large object and place it before all members of the group so that it is clearly visible to everyone. Each member of the group should have a pencil and a piece of paper.

All group members should practice *preliminaries, release excess energy, total relaxation,* locate *body centers,* and *collect energy* for focus on the object.

When each person is ready, clear minds and begin receiving impressions. Each word, thought, and phrase should be written down. Clear your mind when you feel confused or when no impression enters your mind. Check your *gut response* to information from time to time when uncertainty about your own feelings interferes with the information you are receiving.

When every person has finished reading, and all pencils are placed down, then, in turn, verbalize your impressions to each other. If a person is present who has knowledge of the object or its owner, share your information for verification.

Several objects can be used, each comprising the focus for a *reading*, so the members of the group can experience reading objects of various shapes and sizes, time periods, and owners.

DOWSING

Dowsing involves several psychic abilities, the most basic one being *psychometry*. It is the process of locating objects or resources usually buried underground or hidden from sight. A *dowser*, one who performs *dowsing*, holds a *divining rod*, which is a forked stick or pole, in front of his body and parallel to the ground. As he walks forward, his psychometric ability helps him to connect with the energy of the buried object. The *divining rod*, an extension of his hand(s), will dip toward the ground where the object or resource is buried.

Dowsing can be used to discover natural resources otherwise unknown, water, oil, minerals, buried treasure, or artifacts from past civilizations. Farmers and explorers in early times, without the aid of highly developed technical systems, used *dowsing* as a common and natural way to find resources that would better their livelihoods.

Exercise: Dowsing for an Object Outdoors

Find a forked piece of wood of any size to use for your *divining rod*. When choosing the wood, hold it in your hand to see if you feel comfortable with it and to sense if there is any energy inside it before you begin. If you wish to release the energy obtained from the wood, take your hands off the wood and place them on an inanimate object until you feel balanced again. Replace your hands on the wood and sense the energy again. If you need to drain more energy from the wood repeat the procedure.

If you have no wood or other durable natural resources available, use your hands as your *divining rod*. Place them, palms down, extended before you and parallel to the ground. Because you are sensing energy, your hands will respond as connectors to that energy.

While you are preparing your *divining rod,* have another person bury an object, previously decided upon, in a reasonably large area, such as a yard, hillside, or wooded thicket. You should not know the exact location of the buried object, only the approximate parameters of the area surrounding it.

When the person has returned, practice all *preliminaries* and, when ready, pick up your *divining rod,* extend it from your body parallel to the ground and begin walking. Allow your own sensing to lead you around the area. Keep your mind clear so that any information helpful to you will be received. If you become confused or find the *divining rod* remaining fixed and not dipping, relax and repeat the *preliminaries* before beginning again.

Continue *dowsing* until you feel you have found the spot. Dig through the earth until you unearth the object. If you are wrong, clear your mind and, using your *divining rod,* begin again. Repeat this procedure as often as you wish or until you find the buried object.

Exercise: Dowsing for an Object Indoors

The same exercise previously explained can be used when undeveloped land is unavailable or weather does not permit access to outdoor activities.

Follow the same procedures as mentioned in *dowsing* for

an outdoor object; simply have the person bury the object in a large indoor space: a basement, barn, attic, or room. The object can be buried under anything as long as its shape and appearance are concealed. Be sure to bury the object away from objects of the same size or shape.

In this instance it might be useful for the *dowser* to first hold and see the object to gain a sense of its energy before beginning to dowse. This will enable you to distinguish the object's energy from the energy of other objects that may be in the same room.

When you have finished with *preliminaries* and have cleared your mind, begin *dowsing* until the object is found. Depending on space, this exercise as well as *dowsing* for an object outdoors can be conducted by several *dowsers* simultaneously, as long as each person does not interfere with the movements and impressions of another.

DAILY USES FOR PSYCHOMETRY

Aside from *dowsing* for buried treasures or resources, your psychometric abilities can be used in various areas of your life.

Law enforcement agencies and private investigators enlist the help of *psychometrists* to locate missing persons or solve crimes that lack the availability of eyewitnesses or verifiable information. By holding a letter written by the victim, or an article of his or her clothing, or by reading a photograph, a *psychometrist* can give valuable information about the person, the crime, or the assailant involved. Since nonphysical energy is not time oriented, people who have been missing for years or crimes unsolved in the past can be traced in this manner.

Psychometry is increasingly being used in anthropological studies and archeological digs to date artifacts and determine information about cultures that have no living survivors or traceable origins. By holding a pottery shard, rug, tool, or other remnant from the lost society, a *psychometrist* can relate information about the person, tribe, time period, or culture that created the object.

On a personal level, *psychometry* can be used in your daily life. When you go to the library, or bookstore, or magazine stand to find something to read, save yourself time and energy by holding the book or magazine that interests you in your hand to gain a sense of the material between its covers. By allowing impressions to enter your mind, you can decide instantly if the book or magazine is worth reading. If you cannot choose between two books, hold each separately in your hand, and allow your psychometric skills to work for you. If you are pressured by time and must decide instantly, let your *gut response* help you decide which book to choose as you hold them.

If you are deciding which product to buy or researching a field of products for a marketing firm, you can eliminate those products least helpful to you by either standing before them or holding each in your hand and reading them using your psychometric ability. Each *reading* will save you time and extra work.

If you are signing a contract and are not sure of its content, hold the contract in your hand and clear your mind. You might receive information concerning missing clauses or gain a sense of the contract in relation to your work.

If you have lost an earring, or cufflink, or object of importance to you, clear your mind and see what impressions come to you. If you have time and space, practice *dowsing* for the object within the confines of the place where you last saw it. If your pet is missing, hold its collar, or toy, or feeding bowl in your hand and focus on your pet, using your psychometric ability to help you find him.

If you work in a business or are a teacher or student and

need to write an important letter to a specific person, try to locate a photograph of the person or have them give you a business card from their wallet so you can read the person before writing the letter.

If you are an editor or buyer for a company, or wish to purchase an article from a department store, hold the book, product or object in your hand and allow impressions into your mind concerning its value to you.

Psychometry can help you keep in touch with friends and loved ones who live long distances away. Hold the letters they have written or read the photographs sent and allow your impressions to connect you more closely to them.

If you work in personnel or are a member of a computer dating service, hold the picture or handwriting of the person you are interested in and verbalize the impressions that come to mind. *Psychometry* can help you avoid hiring incompetent people and prevent needless encounters with people who are tiresome to you.

Whether you choose a movie from the picture ads in the newspaper, a vacation by holding a travel brochure, a bicycle from a rack of many, a watch, a ring, or even the food you eat, *psychometry* can be of great help to you.

Every time you walk into a supermarket or grocery store and face a row of products, each claiming to have the best benefits for you, hold the box, or can, or envelope in your hand and determine the best product to buy. No amount of advertising, packaging, or promises can overcome your objective psychometric ability.

Whether you use your ability to choose food, solidify a contract, buy and date an antique lamp, discover a hidden road without a map, or find a necklace you've misplaced, your psychometric ability can help you make decisions that will allow you to live more comfortably and save you time and money.

Questions and Answers

If I start to get many impressions when I read a photo of a group of people, how can I focus more clearly on the person I want to read?

When reading a group photograph use the *preliminaries* as often as needed to help you focus clearly on the person you wish to read. If you wish to cover the other people with a piece of paper during the *reading*, do so. This will help give you a simple visual focus. You may find it helpful to look at the person you wish to read and then look away as you allow the impressions to come into your mind without settling your vision on the rest of the picture. This can be done several times during the *reading*, especially when you become confused or find no information coming forth. Your *gut response* will also help you in accessing the focus of your *reading*.

Why would you get more information from one object or photo of a person than another object or photo of the same person?

The reason this occurs is that the first object has probably been used more frequently by the person or owned for a longer period of time by them. Their energy would then be more involved with the object. In reading a particular photograph more easily than another, the first photograph may depict the person more clearly or may have been taken at a time when his or her energy was strong in its vibrations. Another possible explanation for the difference in information is that you, the *psychometrist*, may have been more open and relaxed during the first *reading*(s) so that the information flowed more freely. Your impressions would then be more vivid in that *reading* than the other. This has nothing to do with any of the objects or photographs. It has to do with the focus and openness of the *reader*.

How can I use psychometry *to help me with a job interview?*

Before attending the interview, try to hold a letter requesting the interview, or some correspondence from the person you are to see. If available, find a photograph of the person in a trade magazine or newspaper or company brochure. Read both the letter and photograph, if possible, to give you insight into the person you are to meet so you will be able to provide him or her with the most favorable part of you in the interview. If neither letter nor photograph is available, practice the *preliminaries* before and during the interview to help you feel relaxed, centered, and focused on the questions being asked. If, during the interview, the person gives you a book he or she has written or a brochure or contract, hold the item in your hand while the interview proceeds. Allow whatever impressions you gain to help you during the interview.

If given a choice, is it better to read an object or a photograph of a person?

The choice is yours. One is not better than another. If you feel more comfortable holding an object, or if the photograph is not clearly focused, or your view of the person is obstructed in any way, reading the object would be better. If the object has been passed through many different hands and the photograph is a clear depiction of the person, then the photograph would be better to read. Circumstance and comfort of the *reader* are the determining factors.

How do you read a photograph or object of a deceased person?

A photograph or object of a person who is deceased can

be read in the same way as that of any living person. Their energy is no longer in their body, but it still exists. A *reading* of this type is usually given to a relative or a friend who wishes understanding about the death of the person or about mutual problems still needing to be worked through by the living person. You can, by giving the person objective insights, help them overcome blocks and defenses or painful feelings that may otherwise be carried with them through their lives.

Another reason for using *psychometry* to read a deceased person is to aid relatives or friends in finding lost heirlooms, contracts or important papers. These valuables may be around with no apparent trace of location. By holding a photograph or object or by *dowsing* in the place where they were last seen, a *psychometrist* can help locate important articles otherwise thought irretrievable.

five

THE BODY
AND
THE SPIRIT

Your nonphysical energy, once it enters the body through
its *energy exchange channel*, becomes physically oriented
to help you learn and grow. After it enters your body,
where does it go? And how can you use this energy more
fully in your everyday life?

THE BODY

The physical vessel that helps utilize and direct our nonphysical energy is the body. Bodies come in different
shapes, colors, and sizes, but all have the same functioning
parts: arms, legs, brains, organs, muscles, and cells. If the
body is not physically maintained and nurtured, its activities are hampered. If you do not work in unison with the
body, your talents, including psychic talents, capabilities,
and potential, cannot be physically realized. Without a

constant natural flow of energy, the body is inhibited and unnecessary problems and difficulties are created.

When your nonphysical energy enters your body it centers in your *gut* or *body center*. Here, it merges with your body's physical energy and disperses through your entire physical being. Your *body center* is where both nonphysical and physical energies combine strongly to become one energy. When you go against your *gut response* at any time, you are truly going against your total self. Physical problems can manifest and cause functional disorders throughout your entire body. This lack of harmony at your very core, endured, over a period of time, can limit your potential in any undertaking. By working with your *gut response*, you are working with your combined energy: the total you.

Close your eyes and allow yourself to relax each part of your body as you have done before in *total relaxation*. While you are relaxing, feel your body, part by part, until you feel yourself as a whole body unit. Breathe naturally and move toward your *body center*, focusing on your energies.

You are now inside the place where you live most. Remain inside yourself at your *body center* and experience a sense of your total being. This is your true center. When you allow another person, situation, or need to turn you away from your center, you are betraying your true self. Your body is your home: It always goes with you, protecting you, working for you, and growing with you; it is yours to preserve and cherish.

Allow your focus to move from your *body center* through your body again, feeling each part as you go, until you are ready to open your eyes again. Sit quietly, breathe naturally, and look around you. You are physically separate from every other living being and yet, through your body, you share a basic coexistence. Each body acts as a direct medium to balance and sustain its energy flow.

As a physical being, your human body houses the following resources for your growth:

- The five senses
- Emotions and intelligence
- Memory
- Physical potential
- Half your total consciousness

Your body is the physical representation of your energy on earth. When you leave the earth you return to your energy, leaving the body and its resources behind. As energy you have no need for physical senses, feelings, dates and places in time, nor physical desires and needs, because you are no longer physical. Your consciousness is nonphysical again. Returning to your cloud you merge with all clouds on a nonphysical level.

THE SPIRIT

If, in fact, you need your total energy to live, what then does your nonphysical energy contain?

Your nonphysical energy, or cloud, has a consciousness as well. It is commonly referred to as your *spirit*, or soul, or higher self. It contains your nonphysical resources for your growth. They include:

- Knowing
- Sensing
- Creative and psychic potential
- Sense of universality

89

- Overall learning and free will
- Half your total consciousness

From your *spirit* you derive your wisdom, which is not always related to a physical instance, such as the ability to transcend the moment and relate with understanding and empathy, to all people involved even when they have hurt you. Your nonphysical senses benefit the body senses, allowing you the added use of your innate responses.

Your creative and psychic potential are not limited by the physical, and can be drawn from your *spirit* and used to expand your dimensions. It is from your *spirit,* which merges like a cloud with other *spirits,* that you gain a universal feeling of brotherhood and love for all things. The learning you house with your *spirit* relates to all learnings and can add to your wealth of experience. Rather than isolate one experience from another, your overall learnings can be touched upon and used to enlarge the ever growing knowledge of yourself.

Because all your energy cannot physically fit within the dimensions of your body, some of your consciousness remains on a nonphysical level. This allows you to share yourself on both levels, physically and nonphysically, to gain a balanced perspective of each state of being. Your physical focus can be enhanced by sensing your actions nonphysically, and your nonphysical growing can be added to by the physical learnings you experience. Both body and *spirit* comprise the total you. When your physical life is over, your consciousness is no longer needed in a body and returns to its *spirit* to become one with it on a nonphysical level.

In order to gain the most benefit from your physical life, it is essential that both parts of you, your body and your *spirit,* work together harmoniously. Without this cooperation, your energy flow can become stifled, fragmented, underused, or misaligned.

How can you facilitate this natural harmony? Can it be maintained in a conscious way so that it flows evenly and with direction?

The best way to achieve a working daily harmony between your body and your *spirit* is by communication. Since your body has a consciousness and your *spirit* has a consciousness which when combined, forms the total you, communication can be maintained in a very easy manner.

Communicating with your body and *spirit* is like talking to yourself. You talk to yourself every day, reminding yourself of a task that needs to be done, reprimanding yourself when you do not please yourself, and congratulating yourself when you do. When you are alone, you sometimes carry on a running conversation with yourself, speaking aloud. When you have a specific voice within yourself to focus on, the communication can become clearer and more valuable in accomplishing simple tasks, making important decisions, avoiding needless worry and anxiety, and facilitating your own positive view of yourself.

Your body and your *spirit* are like two people living in the same house, trying to solve problems between them so the daily process of living can run smoothly. As with any two people living together, problems do arise between them. Although they are, for the most part, compatible because they are parts of the same whole, they exist on different levels of yourself. In your house, one person lives on the bottom floor and is used to the ground level experience. The other lives nearest the sky and has little or no perception of the ground below. Through communication, each can give to the other the perspective each is lacking in order to make the house something whole and shared. Although their common bond is their house, each may not feel secure with the other's perspective.

If your *spirit* is not working with your body or is hesitant to trust that level of perception, you will usually find yourself experiencing a lack of direction; feeling lost and repeating situations throughout your life, because you are not able to draw upon your wisdom and overall learning experience. You will feel confused from time to time, off balance in situations, and unable to utilize your psychic and creative abilities in meaningful ways. Relying on half of yourself, you will find yourself reacting like a car with its motor running but without a driver, idling, or coasting until you come to a stop.

If your body is not working with your *spirit,* you will find yourself trying to solve problems or dealing with situations without the sense of time or memory needed to effect any change. You will lack a balance of emotional stability, substituting misdirected feelings for inappropriate situations. You could feel anxious or drained, not having the body allocating energy as you need it. You will find yourself drifting through life without physical focus. Like a car driven by a person who has no sense of the roadway or the mechanics of the vehicle, you will be prone to accidents or quick starts and stops without moving in specific directions toward your goals.

Exercise: Body and Spirit Communication

Find a time and place where you can be alone and quiet. When beginning communication between your body and *spirit,* you may desire a visual focus for yourself. If it is convenient and comfortable for your body, stand or sit in front of a mirror and look at yourself. If you would rather close your eyes when communicating, find a comfortable position for your body to remain in during the exercise.

Release excess energy and practice *total relaxation.* Feel your body once again as a physical being, experiencing all parts of yourself, especially your *body center.*

Ask your body a simple question. For example, ask it if

your energy flow is hampered in any way or if it is having problems releasing or exchanging energy. Focusing on yourself in the mirror or with eyes closed, wait and listen for a reply. Your voice will be a thought inside your mind similar to the way you think. The thought will locate in a specific area inside your head. Listen to your body's entire thought.

If, at first, you do not get a response from your body relax and try again, asking yourself another question if desired. Your body may have been trying to speak to you for a long time and may have built a sense of frustration or anger that has inhibited it. As you might treat any friend, be patient with your body and willing to listen to it. Your body is your closest physical friend. If you are still having difficulty, ask your body a question that is more physically direct, such as, "Why are you always late for work," or, "Why are you so tired all the time?"

When beginning communication with your body, it is best to keep your questions simple so you do not get confused. You are learning to discover your body's voice, not to solve every problem you have in one sitting. Keep asking your body questions until you feel that you have a definite sense in your body's inner voice and where the thoughts locate inside your head.

Breathe deeply and relax yourself again. Facing the mirror or with eyes closed, focus on your *spirit,* or cloud, outside your body. Ask your *spirit* a simple question. You may ask, "Am I blocking the energy coming into my body?" or, "How can I use more of my energy for my psychic abilities?" Listen for an answer.

Your *spirit* also has a voice that will locate in thought(s) inside your head. Your *spirit*'s thoughts will not be directed to the same place inside your head as your body's thoughts. They will locate in another part of your head. If you receive no answer to your question(s), relax, and ask your *spirit* another question, such as, "Are you having trouble working with the body?" or, "Do you sense the *energy exchange channel?"* Continue asking questions until you are familiar with the voice of your *spirit* and where it locates inside your head.

When you have become comfortable with both your body's and your spirit's thoughts, relax again. *Release excess energy* and *collect* your *energy* to focus on your body. Allow your body to now ask your *spirit* a direct question. Wait and listen to the thought response inside your head. After the *spirit* response is completed, allow your body to reply. When this conversation is concluded, allow your *spirit* to ask your body a question and then wait for your body's reply. Continue the dialogue between both parts of you, each responding to or questioning the other, until you have a good sense of both processes.

If you become confused during the dialogue, your *gut response* will help to verify the information itself or the source of the information. You are talking to yourself in the truest sense. Both functioning parts of you, your body and your spirit, are conversing.

Continue communicating and you will find that both your body and *spirit* will respond genuinely and easily to one another, for they are both of the same energy. Once you begin your dialogue, you will soon become more friendly with your body and be able to sense your *spirit* more closely. Without this cooperation, the tension inside you could result in the same difficulties you might encounter with an estranged close friend: anguish, distrust, confusion, resentment, and blindness toward one another.

Through communication, a feeling of well-being and progress can be achieved and continued on a daily basis. Talk to yourself wherever you are, whenever you need to commune with yourself. Your dialogue is private and can be continued at any time throughout your day or evening.

Once you experience your entire self, you will never feel abandoned or alone again.

USES FOR BODY AND SPIRIT COMMUNICATION

Every aspect of your daily life is affected by your inner harmony. If you worked late the night before and have to be alert for an important early morning meeting, before retiring, ask your body to release excess thoughts and energies during sleep, and ask your *spirit* to help your body maintain a focused balance of energy through the meeting.

Each part of you has its own expertise in facilitating health and body maintenance. The body cannot use energy that is not available, nor can the *spirit* pull energy inside the body and distribute it effectively to the body parts. Each needs the other to actualize your balance and harmony.

If you are going to an appointment and are nervous, ask your body to remember its capabilities and to center itself in the *body center*. Ask your *spirit* to help release tensions through the *energy exchange channel*, and allow a sense of knowing to alleviate momentary fears.

If you are staying up late to study or take care of a sick child, ask your body and *spirit* to assist you so that you are not drained by the activities you are enduring. The more you communicate with yourself, the more aware you will be of what each part of yourself has to offer and teach you about your own capabilities. If you face any problem, no matter how serious, and don't know what your *spirit* or body can do to help you, ask them. You will not only remedy the situation, but will gain more knowledge about your own potential.

If you are a doctor performing a serious operation, a lawyer in court, a teacher with a full class schedule, a salesperson or waiter/waitress working a double shift, a seamstress, secretary, laborer; if you find yourself: with a flat tire on the highway, waiting for the train, standing in line at the checkout counter, or having a fight with a neighbor; you can still be comfortable inside yourself and able to deal with the situation(s). If you are run down, agitated, frustrated or sick, you can readily discover the source of your difficulty and relieve it by communicating with yourself. With your *spirit* and your body working together, you always have a friend, in fact, two friends on whom you can always rely.

Questions and Answers

What are some things I can do to improve my listening ability so I can listen better to myself?

Observe yourself with other people and see how you react when they are talking to you. Try listening more carefully to others and appreciate what they have to say. Ask your body to help you listen to others. You will begin listening more closely to your body's responses to what other people are saying. Once you are in touch with your body, it will be easier to listen to your *spirit*. If you still find listening to yourself a problem, ask your body and/or *spirit* to show you, in very tangible everyday actions, what they are trying to say to you. Observe your actions and see, by your *gut response*, if what you observe is the message they are trying to convey. Any time you are unsure about the communication or what part of you is communicating, your *gut response* will verify it for you. In time you will find yourself able to be more introspective and alert to the thoughts within you.

Is is possible to control, increase or decrease the energy flow in my body?

Yes. When working with both your body and *spirit*, you are truly working from the best vantage point for balancing yourself. In fact, if you want to increase your energy for a specific physical activity or long period of time, but your body knows that taking in more energy at this time would be harmful and cause an imbalance, rather than take in the energy it will tell you what is happening and rebalance itself. This gives you an additional perspective when dealing with situations. The same is true for your *spirit*. Working with both parts of yourself will allow you to work with and perceive your entire being.

Can I direct my energy to a specific part of my body if it needs it?

If your feet are tired, your shoulder hurts, your head feels filled with confusion and you have to continue your five-mile hike to the gas station, or your suitcase feels like it has gained ten pounds and your child is crying as you meet the train and find you have the wrong ticket, simply ask your body and spirit to help you alleviate any specific problem you are having inside yourself. The results, when you are communicating freely, are instantaneous and will endure regardless of time or circumstance.

Can my energies be harmful to me at any time? Can they be harmful to anyone else?

Your energies are self contained on a physical level and can affect only yourself. Too much energy will not hurt you, it will only cause you to feel nervous or anxious until it can be relieved by communicating. Lack of energy will cause you to feel drained or listless, but it will not destroy you. Your energy is what helps you grow and live. Even at its most imbalanced state, it will not hurt you, but only cause you momentary discomfort. The energies shared by everyone are beneficial and compatible in aiding the balance and harmony of life.

six

AURAS

Look around you. Everything you see has a color. When you pick a flower, paint a room, choose a coffee cup, buy a car, or shop in the supermarket, color is an important factor. Every day when you put on your clothes, you are choosing colors that make you feel comfortable.

Stand in front of a mirror and look at yourself. What are the colors you are wearing? How do they make you feel? Do they reflect your mood? What are your favorite colors? Do they change as you change your moods about yourself? Do your color choices reflect your view of yourself?

Societies sometimes help us determine our reactions to colors. In early civilizations, colors derived from nature were those most commonly used and seen. All cultures place great importance on color in their spiritual worship. Native Americans, for example, believe the colors blue, white, black, and yellow to be sacred and use them in their healing and religious rituals. Red and gold are significant in the Christian religion, while orange is sacred to many

Eastern religious cultures. Purple and black together tell people in Western society that there has been death and mourning.

When advertising and selling merchandise, color is of major importance. Packaging, hair products, stuffed animals, cooking and eating utensils, food, ribbons, attaché cases, lingerie, even our toothbrushes are made with specific colors. Male and female babies are differentiated in Western society by the colors blue and pink. Schools, clubs, and nations have predominant colors by which to distinguish themselves. Our telephones and even our houses are chosen for their colors.

If color is so important to our physical selves, can the same be true about our nonphysical selves? If our nonphysical energy is part of our physical selves, won't our energies also have color?

On an energy level there is no need for color to define ourselves. When your nonphysical energy combines with your body, it becomes more confined to the limitations of density, light, and form. The result of this transformation of nonphysical energy is an *aura*. It is an emanation of energy from the body which can be seen in color(s). This life energy can be seen or sensed around every living thing: plants, animals, birds, insects, fish, water, natural resources, or human beings. Your *aura* is the physical manifestation of your nonphysical energy.

In ancient times when the earth was free from atmospheric intrusion, *auras* were easily seen and read to determine a person's health and spiritual well-being. Primitive paintings carved in stone were often drawn with radiating lines around the edges of the figures. Religious pictures depicted holy people or angelic figures with halos. These radiating lines or circles of light were representations of the person's *aura*.

Today we can photograph a person's *aura* by using a

specially designed camera and light-sensitized film. This process, first discovered in the Soviet Union, is called Kirlian photography, named after the Russian who developed it. It is used extensively in medical research and scientific investigation. By filming the energy and its colors surrounding an area on a person's body, a clinician or doctor can determine whether that particular body area emanates a different color than the rest of the body and whether that area is disturbed by an interference that the naked eye cannot see. A photograph of this type, unlike an x-ray, has no serious side effects. The *aura* is a natural emanation and needs no radiation to divulge it.

The benefit of reading an *aura* is that it can be broken down into several parts to facilitate insight. There are three basic parts to an *aura*, or energy field, around the body. The first color, closest to the body itself, is called the *physical aura*. It represents the body's physical growth, strengths, and weaknesses. The second color, moving away from the body, is called the *mental or emotional aura*. It reflects the person's emotional moods and mental feelings. This *aura* part is most changeable and fluctuates throughout the day, depending on mental and emotional stimulations. The third part of the *aura*, and the color most distant from the body, is the *spiritual aura*. This reflects the energy of the *spirit* and its development. (See Figure 3.)

All three parts of your energy combine to form your total *aura*. Each part of your energy field can be read separately or can be read in conjunction with each of the others. The colors are not physically separated by a line or space between them and sometimes appear to fuse or change into one another. One color may be more predominant than the others, depending on the development of the person at that time. When giving an *aura reading* you will be able to sense each part of the *aura* and give viable information concerning its relationships to the person you are reading.

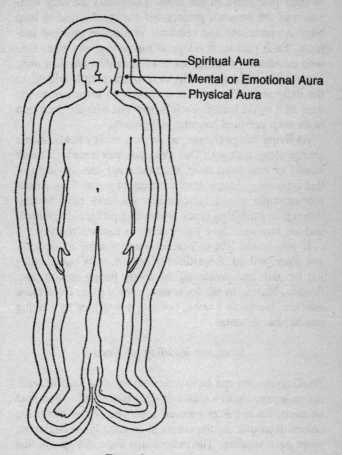

— Spiritual Aura
— Mental or Emotional Aura
— Physical Aura

Figure 3. Types of auras.

There is no judgment or hierarchy involving the colors or their placement in the *aura*. The colors are only indicators of the person's present self and can be read to help alleviate problems and reinforce productive growing patterns. Each person develops at his or her own rate. One who emanates a stronger *spiritual aura* than *physical aura* is not necessarily more enlightened. Learning is relative to the individual. The *aura* of a daisy is as important as the *aura* of a world leader. Each is involved with the evolution of its own personal learning and growth.

As living things change, so do their energy fields. *Auras* change along with you. One week you may emanate a green *mental* or *emotional aura,* the next a red one. An *aura* of this type may change from morning to night. This particular example would indicate that you may have worked through an inhibiting block or solved a problem in yourself and are now resettling your energy to balance yourself.

If you would like to practice *aura reading* at random, any place will do. Regardless of season, walk outside during the day and notice all the living things around you: flowers, leaves, trees, dogs, cats, even a rock. Everything animate, including a book, because it is written by a living person, has its *aura*.

Exercise: Reading an Aura

Reading an *aura* can be experienced within a *psychic reading* or separately as a viable psychic talent. When you read an *aura,* do not stop yourself after you see or sense the colors. Recognizing the colors in an *aura* is the beginning of an *aura reading*. The information about the person that comes to you during an *aura reading* should be verbalized as well. You will find that the information will not only help you define the color you are seeing or sensing, but will add to the insights given.

Sometimes you will actually see a physical color emanating from a person. At other times you will sense the color or colors. One technique is just as valid as the other. The information received about the person that follows will verify and enhance what you are perceiving.

Have your subject sit near a blank wall or area so that the physical surroundings will not distract you. An indirectly lighted place is best for seeing or sensing *auras* because physical shadows may interfere. When you become more proficient in reading *auras,* you will be able to perceive them in any situation, even in semidarkness.

Practice all *preliminaries* before beginning this exercise.

Situate your body in a comfortable position near the person you are reading.

When you are focused and relaxed, look at the outer edge of a part of the person's body: their shoulder, arm, or head. Continue looking at that place on his body until your eyes go out of focus. Without blinking, you will begin to see a distorted view of that surface. Keep your eyes unfocused as long as possible until you see or sense emanations of color from the person's body part.

Verbalize whatever color you see or which comes into your mind. Allow your mind to be clear and repeat any words or thoughts that enter your mind. The colors you see or sense may grow brighter or stronger as the *reading* progresses. You may also begin to see or sense more than one color emanating from the person. Verbalize all impressions as they come to you. If the color(s) recede, remain unfocused on the body part and continue to give information. You will find that the color(s) will return as you continue to examine them.

If you are seeing or sensing nothing, or sense a mixture of colors you cannot define, relax, and continue looking at the body part until the colors become more clear to you. If you find yourself pushing to see a color or are confused, close your eyes or look away from the person for a moment. Look again and allow your eyes to become unfocused or choose another body part on which to focus.

Explore other parts of the body in the same way to note any differences in the *aura* or information you are receiving. If you get tired, or, before shifting focus on another body part, look away from the body, practice *preliminaries,* and begin again.

When sensing or seeing *auras* at first, do not worry about the specific interpretation of the color or the difference between the colors in the *auras.* Your *gut response* will help you clarify what you are experiencing. Trust yourself and allow all impressions to continue to aid you in clarification.

There are many interpretations you can find in books on the subject of *auras* and the meaning of colors. The basis for each *aura reading* you give is your own ability. If you allow yourself to determine the meaning of the *aura* you are seeing or sensing by external charts or cultural derivation, you will interfere with the objectivity of the information you are receiving. For example, if you are reading an *aura* and see black around the person's heart, instead of stopping the *reading* to consult lists and books or to remember the meaning of black in your present culture or the culture of the person you are reading, you should continue with the *reading* to find your own sense of the relationship between the color and the person. Black may relate to independence or the solitude the person is experiencing, which helps to strengthen self. You may come to find, through the information given, that the person has recently been separated from a loved one and black represents sorrow about his loss.

Colors can mean many things in relation to the person being read. Red, which we have come to know as a color of anger or shame, can also represent healing and love. Green reminds us of growth, but yellow can also mean growth and emerging prosperity. The added list of colors and examples of their meaning at the end of this chapter can familiarize you with popular descriptions of colors. Do not limit yourself to these meanings. Verbalize your impressions and find your own sense of the colors you are seeing without preconceptions that might inhibit your ability.

Exercise: Reading Your Own Aura

Reading your own *aura* is an exercise you can do every day. All you need is a mirror, a semilighted room, and your body.

Stand before a mirror at a comfortable distance and, if possible, let the light filter behind you to avoid shadows.

Practice *preliminaries*, clear your mind, and look at the edge of your shoulder or any other part of your body. Keep looking at the same spot until your eyes become unfocused.

The color(s) you are either seeing or sensing are your own *aura*. Allow any impressions or thoughts about the colors or yourself into your mind and verbalize them.

If you sense or see colors emanating from another source, such as a painting or wall in the background, or reflection, change your position or ask your body to help you focus your eyes more clearly on the spot at which you are staring.

Practice reading your *aura* several times during the day to note changes and to familiarize yourself with *aura reading* in several situations. The results you discover may be surprising and productive.

COMPARING AURAS

Since all living things have *auras*, you can read the colors emanating from your favorite pets, plants, or objects. Anything that contains natural ingredients has an *aura*.

Comparing *auras* of specific products can help you as a consumer or business person. It is a quick and efficient way of selecting products that are beneficial to you without having to take time to read labels or study comparison data. If several people have touched or handled the product or book, use your *gut response* and impressions gained to help you distinguish between them.

Exercise: Comparing Auras

Find two books of similar size, two packages of food with natural ingredients (a product totally synthesized will have little or no *aura* because it does not include living energy), two vegetables, handmade pottery, or any objects of comparable size.

Cover each item with a bag or wrapper to hide any physical titles or characteristics.

Place both packages before you, equidistant from each other.

Use all *preliminaries* before beginning the exercise.

Look at one bag, staring at the corner or edge of the object until your eyes go out of focus, and read its *aura*. Verbalize any impressions you may receive in your mind once it has been cleared. Continue until all information has been relayed and all colors have been seen or sensed.

Clear your mind and relax. Practice *preliminaries* if needed.

Look at the other bag and repeat the exercise used for the first bag. Read its *aura* and allow all information to come into your mind about the object.

When you are finished comparing *auras* and information, take the items from the bags and look at them. Compare your physical perceptions with the ones you have received psychically.

Practice this exercise using several items. Make sure that you read the *aura* and give information about each object separately to avoid confusion.

DAILY USES FOR AURA READING

Reading *auras* is an easy way to become a better consumer. You can read auras when choosing plants, flowers, clothing, books, magazines, candy bars, or pets. Your tastes as a consumer will change as you change. Reading *auras* will help you become aware of these changes and select those products which will benefit you.

When you are choosing land to buy or where to plant your garden, use your *aura reading* ability. If you are buying several animals or selecting a puppy from a litter, read its *aura* to find the most suitable animal for you. When deciding on a picnic spot, a mountain to ski down, a campsite, house, apartment, or gift to buy, read its *aura*. When someone you care for is upset or ill, read his or her *aura* to help you give directed attention where needed. If you are having a problem and can't seem to get insight or information, read your *aura* to help you see the difficulty. *Auras* are colorful tools that can give you additional insight when you need it.

POLARIZING YOUR ENERGY FIELD

Auras are useful in other ways. They can help to protect you from danger, physical harm, or illness. You can strengthen the energy you emanate around you to separate you from an unhealthy or dangerous situation. By adding more energy to your *aura* you create a force of energy around you. This shield of energy is called your *aural* or *energy field* and acts like a nonphysical energy shield to ward off that which is physically harmful to you.

The process of creating and enlarging your *energy field* is called *polarization of energy.* With the aid of your body and your *spirit* you can *polarize* your *energy field* by pulsating your nonphysical energy from your *body center,* so it emanates more strongly from your body. All you need to do is communicate with your body and *spirit* and envision your energy filling an arc around your entire body. Strengthen this arc of energy for as long as you prefer. (See Figure 4.)

When you are walking down a street and a dog runs toward you with his teeth bared, or a suspicious looking person is following you, or your opponent in a sporting event is about to collide with you, communicate with your body and *spirit* and allow your *aural field* to polarize, pulsing from your *body center.* You will soon find the dog wandering away, or the person crossing the street or your opponent missing your body by several inches. What you have done is easy to understand. You have filled the space around you with energy. Nothing can penetrate a space that is already full. If you see a person coming toward you whom you would like to avoid, *polarize* your *energy field* to circumvent the encounter.

Exercise: Polarization of Energy

Situate yourself in a place where there are many people: a busy street, supermarket aisle, bus station, or department store for example. When a person moves toward you from the opposite direction, a distance away, practice *prelimi-*

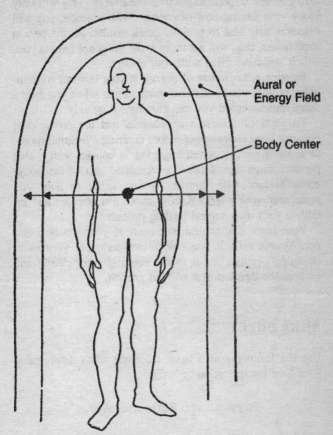

Aural or
Energy Field

Body Center

Figure 4. Polarization of energy.

naries, communicate with yourself, and pulsate energy from your *body center* to fill the space around you. Do not rush yourself or push to *polarize* the *energy.* This will only block your natural flow of energy. With practice, you will discover how best to achieve quick results. As the person approaches, they will naturally avoid the space around you, which you have filled with your energy.

Practice *polarization* of *energy* at your leisure, communicating with your body and *spirit* so that when you face a dangerous situation you can eliminate it quickly.

To ward off illnesses or diseases that are contagious, *polarize* your *energy field* before entering a hospital room, or a classroom, or when engaging in contact with a sick person. Since germs affect a weakened part of the body, communicate with your body and *spirit* to help you strengthen your *energy field* to avoid disturbances and facilitate your own natural healing process.

Your *aura* is a natural extension of your physical and nonphysical self. It is a colorful reflection of your ever-changing beauty. Use it to see yourself more clearly and witness the development of your growth.

AURA SHEET

Use the following as a basic reference when determining your own interpretation of Auras:

PHYSICAL AND EMOTIONAL AURAS

A. Physical Growth

White   —cleansing
Light Green   —stubbornness, firmness, earthly
                       calm

Bright Green	—new growth
Deep Green	—continuing growth
Yellow	—new growth

B. Emotional or Mental Growth

Light Blue	—balance, strength, peace, harmony
Bright Blue	—tranquility, harmony
Navy Blue	—independence, self assurance
Pink	—healing, affection, explosion of feeling
Red	—aggression, sexuality, simplicity, cheerfulness
Deep Maroon	—health, balance of energy
Bright Yellow	—confidence
Golden Yellow	—creativity, spirituality, wisdom
Grey	—old wisdom, calmness, simplicity
Black	—freedom, independence, protectiveness
Brown	—stability
White	—release, inspiration

SPIRITUAL AURA

Clear	—calmness, essence, being
Milky White	—cleansing, new growth
Gold	—attainment of wisdom
Blue	—serenity, tranquility
Purple	—oneness, unity
Opalescence	—wisdom attainment

Questions and Answers

Will color blindness affect aura reading?

When you use your psychic abilities you are not confined to physical limitations. If you are color blind, you can read *auras* clearly by relying on your sensing of the color rather than physically seeing it. If you do see the *aura* and cannot differentiate colors, the information you are receiving about the color or the person in relation to the *aura* will give you exactly what you need for the *reading* to be accurate and productive.

Is it possible that two people might see two different colors when reading the same aura?

Two people may see different colors in the same *aura*. One person may be seeing or sensing the person's *emotional aura* and the other may be seeing the *physical aura*. Since colors tend to blend, it is possible that one or both people are seeing a combination of colors and reading them as one color. The information that accompanies the reading of the color is important to define and clarify insight gained through color perception.

Do animals see auras?

Animals also have the ability to see *auras*. Since they sense rather than feel, they may sense the energy and react to it rather than define it by color. Animals will sense fusion of energy or the emanations of energy from people, areas, and other living things. That is why a dog or cat, without relying on their physical senses, will avoid potential dangers, such as holes or barriers in a yard, before they actually encounter them.

Can I read a person's aura *in total darkness?*

Once you become experienced with reading *auras*, you

will be able to sense and read them wherever you are. Your nonphysical energy is not relegated to the perimeters of light or dark and the colors are not pigmented in a physical way. When beginning to read *auras*, a partially lighted area is best to avoid shadow distractions. Once you are accustomed to your own process you will be able to read *auras* in bright sunlight or darkness.

Can polarizing energy *prevent me from experiencing situations that I might think are harmful, but could be helpful to me?*

If you *polarize* your *energy* in any given situation to avoid a potentially helpful encounter you will find that the same situation or a similar situation will arise again for you. Nothing is fixed and the opportunity for you to grow will present itself to you again.

seven

PSYCHIC HEALING

A kind word, a thoughtful touch, a loving caress can help the body feel better. Psychic healing is a process of adding energy to the body's own energy to help it heal itself and reassume its own natural harmony. Medicine, acupuncture, spinal manipulation, and surgery help to rectify body ailments, but it is the body itself that ultimately does its own healing.

Western society has come to recognize health care through scientific means and technological procedures; without your energy working within the body, healing is limited, regardless of sophisticated techniques and precision oriented tools. Most primitive societies and past civilizations throughout the world have shared a basic natural technique used in *psychic healing: laying on of hands.*

When a *psychic healer* uses *laying on of hands,* the *healer* places his or her hands upon the ailing person's body and allows nonphysical energy to pass through them into that body. The ill body uses this energy to add to its own to help heal itself.

People become ill for many reasons. Some illness is based on organic disfunction, or hereditary traits, or accidental occurrences. Other illness is caused by stress, environment, or the person's own conscious or unconscious mistreatment of his body. If you are not in harmony with your body and *spirit,* and therefore hinder your changing and growing, or hold yourself back so as to block your progress, emotions such as anger, resentment, sorrow, and frustration may, over a period of time, build inside you without an outlet for release. When your body cannot house these energies that disturb its balance, it becomes ill. When the chaos inside your body builds to a great extent, it can debilitate your body and cause you to become bedridden.

In some cases, illness or disease becomes a long-term malady when a person refuses to heed body signals of distress or tension and continues adding counterproductive energy to affect the body balance. This situation can progress to terminate the health of the body and cause death. Sickness is not punishment or lack of worthiness. It is a sign from the body that something is wrong, that your energy balance is off, and that you are ignoring some vital insights about yourself and your possible relation to the world around you.

People do not become terminally ill because they are ignorant or purposefully neglectful of themselves. Some terminal illness is simply due to a continuation of ways of living, or thinking, or being that have become destructive to your body health.

There are cases of people who have been diagnosed and treated for terminal illness, who have reversed their condition and gone on to lead healthy and productive lives. This occurs when the person has recognized certain blocks, or fears, or tensions in himself and has begun to release them and change his patterns of growing. The natural body balance has been reinstated and the body can then help itself heal and be well again.

People who want to become well because they do not want to be sick have a hard time rebalancing body energy. The focus is a negative one and can reinforce impediments to health. Changing one's attitudes about oneself would give focus to a feeling of ability and worthiness to get well and help surpass anger and fear about an illness. One can deal freely with the problems and attitudes that may have caused the illness, rather than focusing on the illness itself. When you involve yourself in your healing process, you can use the trained expertise of others to facilitate your healing. The ability to heal yourself first lies within you.

PSYCHIC HEALING

Psychic healing has sometimes been confused with *faith healing*. *Faith healers* may use *laying on of hands*, but usually they incorporate it within a religious oriented ceremony or ritual. *Psychic healing* is neither bound to nor opposed to any religion. It is a universal method of transferring energy we all share through one body to another.

People have found that a gentle touch from one person to another can help change the way they are feeling. Petting an animal provides an outlet for loving and peace. *Laying on of hands* expands this sharing to help the body maintain a sense of wellbeing.

Psychic healers work in conjunction with medical practitioners in hospitals and hospices throughout the world. In England, *psychic healers* help doctors treat every major type of ailment seen in a hospital setting. In California, New York, and several other states, nurses are being trained in *laying on of hands* to add to their medical schooling.

Terms such as *unconditional touch, holistic healing,* and *touch healing* are used to describe methods that include *laying on of hands* to facilitate the healing process.

In several countries, including Mexico and Puerto Rico, healers perform *psychic surgery.* During this process, a medical operation is performed without using physical instruments to open the body. The *psychic surgeon* uses his hands to reach into the body energy and eliminate the energy of the tumor, ruptured appendix, or broken bone. Although still in its early discovery stages, *psychic surgery* has produced conflicting results, some verifiable and others totally fraudulent.

When you have to see any professional about your health, a distinguished heart surgeon or respected *psychic healer,* understand his ability and personality before having him treat your body. Whatever their prognosis or suggested treatment, this only aids in your healing process. Your body is your responsibility, not theirs.

Your body is a physical instrument. It is your vehicle, through which you use your energies. In order to treat your body in a holistic manner, you should use all of the tools available to you in effecting positive results. Its care and maintenance should be shared with trained and caring people in the health profession, who can treat it physically, and with healers who are loving and skilled to affect it nonphysically.

Medical people, whether trained in conventional or homeopathic techniques, are knowledgeable about the physical mechanics and care of the body. *Psychic healers* are skilled in working with the body's energies, not with its physical structure. When both types of treatment are used, a person can be aided greatly in relieving symptoms and causes of the illness, and in maintaining balanced body health. A doctor or medical person and a *healer* complement, rather than replace, each other. Without your help and responsibility for your body, you limit their potentialities to assist you.

You don't have to be physically ill to be healed. An emotional problem may be causing you anxiety or depression. Before the energy becomes destructive inside you and causes an imbalance of energy that might lead to physical illness, work along with a trained therapist and/or a skilled *healer* to help free yourself of emotional blocks or fears that cause this disturbance inside you. The energy transferred by the *healer* can facilitate your insights, which can be worked through in dialogue with the therapist. Neither person can affect the blocks or change your patterns if you are not willing to do so yourself. They can only assist you in reassuming your healthy body balance.

BODY CHANNELS

Your physical body houses several channels that can aid you in your healing process. Your body uses these channels naturally every day to help maintain its natural flow of energy. You can help facilitate your energy flow by being more aware of, and using these channels consciously.

RELEASE CHANNEL

The *release channel* is a passageway that allows extra body energy, that cannot be drained through extremities, to leave your body. If you feel energy buildup, needless worry, anxiety, depression, confusion, or overstimulation, you can expend this energy through your *release channel*. Any energy your body needs to use for its growth will stay with you. It is not a way of ridding yourself of your own energy or responsibility for growing. It is a functional way to get

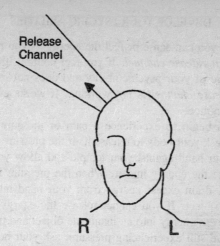

Release
Channel

R   L

Figure 5a. Release channel.

rid of large amounts of energy that the body cannot use. (See Figure 5a.) If you are right-handed, envision a pathway leading outward from your right temple area. If you are left-handed, the pathway is located at your left temple area. This pathway is your *release channel*. If you are ambidextrous you will discover where your *release channel* lies by using the following exercise.

Exercise: Experiencing the Release Channel

Visualize the area around your right temple (left temple if you are left-handed) opening like a pathway away from you.

Practice *preliminaries* and communicate with your body to help release energy.

Open your hand, and place it, palm facing your head, a few inches from your temple area. Allow your hand to remain in this position for a few moments.

See if you can sense or feel the energy as you release it from your *release channel*. If you feel nothing, this is not a measure of your psychic ability and does not mean that your *release channel* is not working. It works every day without notice.

If you begin to experience a pain or pressure at your temple, ask your body to release it. If the pressure persists, place your hand against your temple and allow your body to release the energy into it. When the pressure has been released, drain excess energy from your hand into an inanimate object. If you cannot release the energy at first, drain excess energy into an inanimate object and try again. If you are still experiencing pressure, ask your body what the cause might be. Working along with your body, you will be able to alleviate it.

When you have finished sensing your *release channel*, remove your hand and allow any excess energy to be drained into an inanimate object if you haven't done so already.

If you are ambidextrous, try sensing energy from each temple separately and allow your *gut response* to help you determine on which side your *release channel* is located.

Let go of energy through your *release channel*, throughout the day, even when you are conversing with someone. Focus the pathway outward and allow your body to release any excess energy. Use your *release channel* before sleeping to ensure a peaceful night's rest.

HEALING CHANNEL

The channel located at the temple opposite your *release channel* is your *healing channel*. (See Figure 5b.)

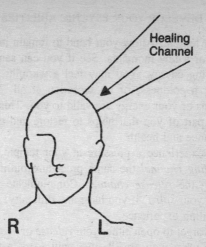

Figure 5b. Healing channel.

It is located at your left temple if you are right-handed; your right temple if you are left-handed. Once you have located your *release channel*, the *healing channel* is easy to find for those who are ambidextrous.

When you are healing another person or if you want to heal yourself, open your *healing channel* inward to allow more energy to aid the healing process. This nonphysical energy is readily available and compatible with all people since, nonphysically, we share our energies. Your healing energy flows naturally into your body as you need it. When you work with it consciously you can increase your ability to heal yourself and others.

Exercise: Experiencing the Healing Channel

Visualize the area surrounding your left temple (right temple for left-handed people) opening like a pathway toward you. Place your open hand, palm facing you, a few inches from your temple. Allow your hand to remain in the same position for a few moments. See if you can sense or feel your healing energy. You may feel a warmth, a tingling sensation, a coldness, or no sensation at all. Your own perceptions of your energy are valid to you. This energy is a natural part of you that helps to restore and effect your body balance and health.

If you experience a pressure at your temple, repeat at your *healing channel* the same procedure outlined in experiencing the *release channel*. Communicate with your body and your *spirit*, if you have any difficulty, to aid you in the healing experience.

If you forget to open either your *release* or *healing channel*, even when you are ill, they will work naturally for you like all of your other body functions. When you work with them consciously, you can maximize the positive effects of your energy upon yourself and others.

FOCAL CENTER

Another body channel that is useful in the healing process also is located in your head. It is called the *focal center* and is centered in the middle of your forehead, equidistant from your eyebrows. This space, often referred to as your *third eye*, is where you send out your healing energy. (See Figure 5c.)

By using your *focal center*, you can channel healing energy to any part of another person's body. Your *focal center*, along with your *release* and *healing channels*, can be used when healing yourself or others. An added benefit occurs when you use your *focal center*. Sending your non-physical healing energy through it, you can heal other people who are not able to be physically present for the

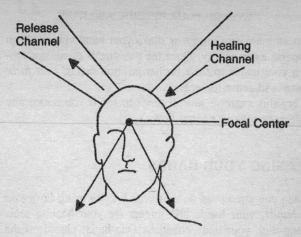

Figure 5c. Focal center.

healing. This energy, not subject to physical limits, can be sent thousands of miles to a person to help him heal himself.

Exercise: Experiencing the Focal Center

Release excess energy into an inanimate object. With eyes opened or closed, visualize your *focal center* opening like a pathway outward. Place your open palms, side by side, a short distance from your *focal center* so that they are facing you. Sense or feel the energy coming from your *focal center.* Allow your hands to remain in position until you have sensed the energy.

If you feel blocked or experience a pressure or pain at your *focal center,* place the palm of one hand, face down, on your *focal center.* Allow the energy blocking or causing you pain to be drawn into your hand. When the pain has lessened, withdraw your hand and *release excess energy*

123

into an inanimate object or shake your hand vigorously to disperse extra energy. Once the pressure is eliminated, return your hands to their former position facing your *focal center* and sense the energy.

Try this exercise several times to see if you notice any difference in your energy flow.

SENSING YOUR HANDS

When you attempt to do a *psychic healing* using *laying on of hands,* your hands and fingers are your healing tools along with your body channels. One hand, placed on the body, usually radiates healing energy into the body. The other hand, placed on the body, draws excessive energy from the body in a way similar to that in which your body channels release and accept energy for you. For some *healers,* the energy will radiate and withdraw from one or both hands simultaneously. For other *healers,* the energy will radiate and release alternately from the same hand, while the other hand will only release energy. Each person will discover that there is no set way of *psychic healing* and every experience will teach each person the best way to work with the healing process.

Exercise: Sensing Energy Through Your Hands

Release excess energy through your hands and feet. Relax your body. Communicate with your body and your spirit to help you focus on the exercise.

Open your *release channel* outward and release any residual excess energy through it.

Open your *healing channel* inward and allow the healing energy to come into your body.

Open your *focal center* outward and allow your energy to flow until you feel or sense it to be clear and open.

Place your open palm, facing you, about two or three inches from your *focal center*. Sense the energy from your hand with your *focal center*. Is it radiating energy or withdrawing it? Does your hand tingle? Does it feel warm or cold? Can you sense the direction of the energy as it comes through your hand? Allow your hand to remain relaxed in this position until you have gained a sense of your energy.

If you find yourself trying too hard to feel or sense the energy, take your hand away from your *focal center* and *release* all *excess energy* into an inanimate object and through your *release channel*. Focus yourself on a simple task until you feel ready to try the exercise again. You are practicing to become familiar with your healing process which may be a new experience to you. If you are confused about your energy flow, try to discover what you might be doing to interfere with it by communicating with your body and/or *spirit* to locate how and why you interfere with yourself. Your *gut response* will also help you discover ways in which you block yourself and your energy flow.

Repeat the same exercise using your other hand. Do you feel energy radiating from your hand or coming into it? Is your hand warm or cold to you? Can you sense your energy? Allow your hand to remain in this position before your *focal center* until you have determined the way your energy is flowing. If you do not sense the energy flow, repeat the same procedure described in the last paragraph.

If both hands sense or feel as if they are radiating and receiving energy you may feel a push and pull of energy simultaneously or experience a tingling sensation. It may, at first, be difficult to differentiate between the energy flows. One hand may be receiving and radiating while the other may be radiating only. Practice sensing both hands with your *focal center* until you discover your own process of *healing*.

LAYING ON OF HANDS

When a *psychic healer* assists a person with his or her own healing process, *laying on of hands* is used. Each hand is placed on the person's body and, using the *focal center*, the *healer* allows healing energy to pass through one or both hands to enter the person's body. Excess energy is released into one or both hands of the *healer* from the person's body to restore a balanced energy flow.

Before any attempt to heal anyone, the person being healed should consult with or be seen by a medical practitioner. Working in conjunction with a trained medical person as well as a skilled *healer* will afford the best results. As a *psychic healer*, your responsibility is to allow energy and information to flow through you to the best of your ability. It is the responsibility of the person being healed to use all benefits to aid him in his own healing process. A *psychic healer* does not take the place of a medical person, nor does a trained medical person take the place of a *psychic healer*. When used jointly they enable the person's body and spirit to resume balance and harmony, provided the person is willing to cooperate.

When doing a *psychic healing*, best results can be achieved by having the person being healed work along with you. The more aware they are of body processes and communications, the more they will be able to facilitate physical healing after the *psychic healing* has concluded.

If a person does not wish to be healed, you have no right to heal him. Whether you approve or not of the way the person is dealing with his illness, you have no right to interfere with the way he has decided to grow or not grow.

Your *healing* will be most effective if the person's body and *spirit* are participating. Because of this cooperation, the energy shared will be blocked or under-utilized. It will work with him in the best possible manner, because he will be participating fully in healing himself.

If a person is hesitant or apprehensive, but wants to be healed, explaining the process of *laying on of hands, releasing excess energy*, and *body communication* will help reduce any fears. It is true that you can heal someone against his wishes, but when this is done you find, in most instances, that the same illness or another like it will develop for the person at a later date. The cause of the initial illness has not been dealt with; only the symptoms have been relieved. The person will, again, have the opportunity to look at and resolve the problem or ignored block that caused the initial illness.

When healing a cooperative person, symptoms may become greater during or after the *healing*, before starting to diminish. Alert the person you are healing to this possibility to prevent unnecessary worry. The condition may reverse itself or manifest more intensely before the body begins to heal, because healing is a natural process. If you have ever had a pimple or an infection, you may have noticed that before it began to disappear, it had to come to a head, burst, and then heal. This is exactly the same thing that happens when you perform a *psychic healing*. The energy helps bring the problem or illness to the forefront and then aids in removing it so that the body heals itself.

There is no need for preconditioning a person once you have explained the healing process to him. Within the course of a *psychic healing*, some people will sense the energy entering and leaving the body; some will feel warm or cold or tingling sensations; some people will sweat, and others will feel nothing at all. This means only that some people are more sensitive to energy sensations than others.

Let the *psychic healing* prove its worth beyond the moment for best results.

Since your own body is a part of the healing process you will also benefit from a *psychic healing* you are giving. The energy that comes through you can help you with your own insights and growth.

Exercise: Laying On of Hands

Allow the person you are healing to be in a relaxed and comfortable position beside you. If they are seated or are lying down, you should be able to have access to all parts of the person's body. If you cannot determine the best position for them to assume during the *psychic healing,* let your *gut response* and the person's physical discomfort, if any, help you.

If the person wants to participate fully with you during the healing process, ask him to *release excess energy* so that you do not absorb any unnecessary energy. If you have time to instruct him about body channels, and body and spirit communication, it will help him enrich his own healing.

With or without the person participating at the same time, practice *preliminaries,* communicate with your body and *spirit,* and open your body channels.

When you are ready, open both hands and place them near the person's body in a relaxed fashion. Let your hands naturally move toward the part or parts of the person's body they are most drawn to regardless of the prominent area of discomfort. For example, the neck area may feel painful, but you may want to place both hands on the right hip during the entire *healing* or move your left hand along the shoulder and upper neck region while the right hand remains on the hip. You may move both hands to a different area of the body or touch separate areas of the body as you feel or sense them. You may want to place one hand on the body only for a while or use one hand during the entire *healing*.

You may not want to touch the body at all, but, rather, place your hands near the body, sensing and working with the person's energy field or *aura*. You may want to massage certain parts of the body with your hands and fingers or project the healing energy to them through your *focal center* without touching the body at all. As you begin to develop your own comfortable method of *laying on of hands*, experiment to find which way is best for you. Each *healing* will be different. Your hand positions are not as important as your ability to send energy clearly to the other person. There is no right or wrong way when healing. An honest, open transmission of energy is your intended goal.

As the energy comes through you into the other person you may feel a tingling sensation in your hands or body, a warmth, coldness, sense of energy flow, other reactions, or nothing at all. The person you are healing may feel all of these reactions, some of them, or nothing at all. Feelings do not measure the worth of the *healing*, nor do they indicate its effectiveness. You will find that the more *healings* you do, the more similarities and differences will occur.

HEALTH READING

During the *psychic healing*, as the energy is being transferred to the person, clear your mind and allow any impressions coming to you to be verbalized the same way you did when giving a *psychic reading* or *aura reading*. This *health reading*, in addition to the transfer of energy, can be resourceful to the person and can help him deal with physical and emotional problems related to the illness. The energy you are transferring is helping to eliminate a block that is stifling a balanced energy flow. With added insight given, the person has an opportunity to understand and work through the problem without continual physical or emotional suffering.

Do not edit any information that is coming to you. Allow all insights, like the energy you are sending, to flow and develop. The focus for a *health reading* is based on the person's physical problems, but if any other information is forthcoming, share it in full with the person. The insights are coming to you for a reason and will help the person's present knowledge of himself and allow him to avoid other physical repercussions of the illness. Stay focused on maintaining an open and honest attitude during the *health reading* and your abilities will be used to their best advantage.

If, at any time during the *health reading* or *psychic healing,* you become confused or overwhelmed by energy or information, relax your body and center yourself at your *body center.* If you need to take your hands from the person, *release excess energy* into an inanimate object, *collect* your *energy,* and allow your channels to open again. Trusting your *gut response,* place your hand(s) on a part of the person's body you feel drawn to and begin again. Repeat this process at any time during the *psychic healing.* If you find yourself blocking information, follow the same procedure for resuming any *reading:* repeat *preliminaries,* communicate with your body and *spirit,* and clear your mind. The physical contact of your hands upon the person's body or energy field will help you to maintain your focus.

The person being healed may contribute what he or she is physically experiencing during the *psychic healing.* The feedback given, although optional, will help you if the person is having difficulty with the energy coming in, or is experiencing any discomfort during the *healing.*

Do not program yourself for particular results. A person may feel worse, at the time of the *healing,* before feeling better. The body heals itself naturally, building the problem before it relieves it. Let the results of your *psychic healing* stand by themselves. The energy will continue to work inside the person long after the *psychic healing* has concluded.

You will know when to end the *psychic healing:* if there is a sense of termination or there is nothing more coming to you in the form of energy or information. If you are unsure about ending a *psychic healing,* take your hands away from the person, clear your mind and try the procedure again to see if more information or energy is coming forth from you.

There is no limit to the number of *psychic healings* you can do. Since the energy works with the body's own natural timing, it is best to allow some time to pass between *psychic healings* for the energy to continue to work. If you feel that the person would benefit from more than one *psychic healing,* you may suggest, depending on the ailment, a schedule of *healings* over a period of time. All timetables for *psychic healings* should be mutually agreed upon.

When you have completed the *psychic healing,* keep your *release channel* open to expel any residual energy your body may have absorbed during the *healing.*

During or immediately after a *psychic healing,* some *psychic healers* may feel or sense the person's physical symptoms. Do not be alarmed if such sensations appear in your body as if they are your own. It does not mean that you are becoming ill. You are only receiving the sensation of the illness, not the illness itself. This is, for some *psychic healers,* a useful tool which enables them to identify problem areas that they might not otherwise have been able to sense or detect. It can also help the *psychic healer* determine the best position, time, or duration for the *healing* as well as give focus to information during the *health reading*.

Once the symptoms are felt or sensed, they can be readily eliminated from the *psychic healer*. Simply ask your body to relieve itself of all symptoms that are not yours. Open your *release channel* and *release excess energy* through your hands into an inanimate object. The symptoms will disappear as quickly as they surfaced.

BASIC PSYCHIC HEALING

Psychic healings are not used to just make you feel good. When needed, they help maintain an even energy flow and bring problems to the surface even when there is no physical pain or disturbance in the body to accompany them. By utilizing this healing energy, you can break through blocks and defenses that blind you, bringing solutions and added insight to help you look at yourself and grow. *Healing* can also be used as a body cleanser or to give an added boost to eliminate accumulated energy that causes imbalance.

Each time you heal yourself or others this energy facilitates growth and will help bring to the forefront, any problems you may be housing inside yourself, even those that are not evident to you.

A *basic healing* can be used anytime when you do not get a strong sense of where to place your hands on a person or yourself during a *psychic healing,* or when you want to effect or maintain a steady body balance of energy. Simply place your hands, one each on your *body center* and *focal center*, to distribute healing energy to all parts of the body.

Exercise: Basic Healing on Self or Another Person

Since you do not have to be physically ill to use healing energy, you may use the *basic healing* technique to help maintain body energy balance and flow.

Release excess energy, practice *total relaxation,* and *collect* your *energy,* communicating with your body and spirit to help you with your *basic healing.*

Situate your body or the other person in a comfortable position.

Open your *release channel.* When ready, open your *healing channel* and then your *focal center.* Locate your *body center.*

When all body channels are open and working, place one hand, palm open, against the *focal center.* Place the other hand, palm open, against the *body center.*

Follow all suggestions for *laying on of hands* and *health reading* during a *basic healing.*

Be sure to *release* any *excess energy* before and after the *basic healing* to allow your body the most benefit from the *healing.* If you forget to release energy, your body will eliminate any excess energy naturally over a period of time.

Basic healing can be used whenever you wish to enrich yourself with healing energy. Dealing with any problems that surface during the *basic healing* is a personal decision and the possibility of them arising during or after the *healing* should be known.

If you are tired or drained, you may use *basic healing* to help you balance your energy. If you want to direct the energy to heal a specific body part, use your *focal center* or ask your body to help you isolate the energy to that body part.

AURA HEALING

Another way to affect your body energy balance or heal a specific area of your body is *aura healing*. Healing one's *aura* involves sending energy through your hands or *focal center* to the *aura* that surrounds the person's body. By adding healing energy to the energy field or *aura* you also affect the flow of energy inside the body. *Aura healing* can be used by itself or in conjunction with *psychic healing* to aid in the healing process.

Exercise: Aura Healing

Repeat all steps suggested in *laying on of hands* exercise: *preliminaries*, body and *spirit* communication, opening body channels.

Look at a part of the person's body that is painful to him and allow your sight to become unfocused in order to sense, or see his *aura*.

Instead of placing your hand(s) on the body, allow them to remain on that part of the *aura* you are perceiving, or move them along the *aural field* surrounding the person's body, sending and releasing energy to it.

Clear your mind and allow all information concerning color(s) and parts of the *aura* you are perceiving to add insight about the problem area. Verbalize any additional information or impressions coming to you about the person.

The *aura healing* is over when little or no energy and information is coming forth. Practice *aura healing* on several people to explore your own best way of sending and receiving energy and impressions.

If you wish to perform an *aura healing* on yourself, stand in front of a full length mirror and repeat the above exercise using your own body. It is a natural and objective way of determining problem areas and restoring body balance.

Whatever form of *psychic healing* you prefer, each can benefit all living things. The more you practice with your healing ability, the more readily it will be available for you to use.

LONG DISTANCE PSYCHIC HEALING

Healing energy, since it is nonphysical, is not restricted by space or time except when used inside the physical body. It can travel over mountains, oceans, through rooms, telephone wires, and letters. When a person is physically present the healing energy can be transferred directly from one person to another. When this is not possible, healing energy can be sent by using a possession, photograph, telephone or even the person's name to connect you to him.

If a person is sick at home, in a hospital, or nursing home, *long distance psychic healing* can be used to help promote the healing process. If your child is away at camp and is frightened or unhappy or has contracted a bad case of poison ivy, hold the telephone receiver and use it as your connector for *long distance psychic healing*. The energy will continue to work long after the *healing* is concluded.

Exercise: Long Distance Psychic Healing

Repeat *preliminaries*, communicate with your body and *spirit* to aid in cooperation, and open *release channel*, *healing channel*, and *focal center*.

Follow all instructions for *laying on of hands*, using the telephone receiver, or photograph, letter, or possession in place of the body. To facilitate the process when using the telephone, have the person practice *preliminaries,* and open all body channels while holding the receiver. If you are using a possession or photograph, establish a mutually acceptable time for the *healing* beforehand to aid the healing process. Focus on the possession, photograph, or your sense of the person to direct the healing energy. You may want to move your hands on or around the object, during the *healing* as you would do when performing a *psychic healing* or *aura healing* in person. As long as you are relaxed and open to the energy flow and information coming to you, the *healing* will continue to work.

When giving a *long distance healing* without the availability of a connector to the person, or if you feel uncomfortable using a photograph, object, or name for focus, send all healing energy through your *focal center* to the person's body and *aura.*

After *preliminaries,* communication with body and *spirit,* and all body channels are opened, clear your mind. Visualize the person or name of the person inside your mind. Proceed to send healing energy through your *focal center* to that person.

When the *healing* is finished, call the person for feedback about the *healing* so that you can decide whether additional *healings* are needed. Experiment with your *healings* to discover your best way of sending healing energy.

HEALING CIRCLE

If more than one person is available to perform a *healing,* a group of people can join to form a *healing circle.* The energy generated by the *healing circle* can add greater input of energy to the person being healed. A *healing circle* can be used when a practiced *psychic healer* is not available or wishes additional help with the *healing.* The person being healed may or may not be present when using a *healing circle*.

Exercise: Healing Circle with the Person Present

Situate the person in the middle of the circle in a comfortable and relaxed position. All *psychic healers* within the *healing circle* should stand or be seated around the person, at a comfortable distance from him.

Each person, including the person to be healed, should follow *preliminaries*. Communicate with body and *spirit*, open all body channels: *release channel, healing channel,* and *focal center*.

Those in the *healing circle* can then join hands, when ready, with the persons beside them, encircling the person to be healed.

If necessary, the group should decide upon the area of the person to be focused on during the *healing*. Otherwise allow healing energy to flow through all hands and *focal centers* toward the person in the center of the *healing circle*.

If the energy becomes too great for any member of the group during the *healing circle*, simply release hands with the people beside you, step out of the circle, and rejoin the hands of those people who were on either side of you. Once outside the *healing circle*, *release excess energy* through your hands into an inanimate object or shake them vigorously to release energy accumulated. Open your *release channel* and enlist your body's aid in restoring your body energy balance.

If the *healing circle* members wish to have physical contact with the person in the center during the *healing*, the same basic procedure for *healing circle* can be repeated with this variation.

The *healing circle* initially should be as close as possible to the person being healed in its center. After practicing *pre-*

liminaries and body and *spirit* communication, open all body channels. All members should join hands except the two members closest to the person's body part or *focal* and *body centers*. One person should place his free hand upon the body part or *focal center*. The other person should place his free hand upon the body part or *body center*. The *healing circle* is performing a *laying on of hands* or *basic psychic healing* using the group energy as a whole to act as the *psychic healer*. As the *healing* continues the two people touching the person's body can move their hands accordingly upon the body or *aura* to advance the body healing.

If desired, the members of the *healing circle* can extend their hands before them, palms outward toward the center person, instead of joining hands. Sending energy to the person through their hands and *focal centers*, they can also aid in the healing process.

Before beginning a *healing circle*, the best means in which to send healing energy to the center person should be established so that all members participate equally for the duration of the *healing* in whichever variation is chosen. Switching variations of the *healing circle* during a *healing* may disrupt the energy flow and disturb the focus of the *healing*. A time period for the *healing* also should be established before beginning. If no time limit is decided upon, the *healing circle* can be concluded when members of the *healing circle*, upon completion, step out of the circle, rejoining the hands of those beside them, until the *healing circle* is diminished and no longer able to function.

Any and all information gained by any member of the *healing circle* should be verbalized to the person being healed. Responses from the person about the energy felt or sensed can contribute to the growth of the *healing circle* in its ability to promote healing.

Exercise: Healing Circle Without the Person Present

If a person cannot be physically present for a group *healing,* but wishes to be healed by a *healing circle,* the same suggestions as for the previous exercise apply. Substitute, in place of the person, a photograph, object, handwriting or person's name on a piece of paper, face up, in the center of *healing circle.* Any one of these items serves as a physical connector to the person being healed.

If there is more than one absent person to be healed, all photographs or names should be placed equidistant from each other in the center of the *healing circle.* If desired, the name of each person can be spoken aloud for focusing before the healings begin.

The *healing circle* or variations of the *healing circle* can be used to help heal all people absent. Be sure to practice *preliminaries,* communicate with body and spirit, and open all body channels before attempting the *healing.* When finished, *release excess energy* into inanimate objects and through *release channels.*

After the *healing circle* is finished, one person should be selected to speak to the person(s) being healed to gain response to the *healing* for future development of the *healing circle.*

DAILY USES FOR PSYCHIC HEALING

Healing is a natural way to comfort or help anyone you love. By healing someone you invariably receive the benefit of the healing energy so that the experience is mutually beneficial. Many people in health professions—doctors, nurses, physical therapists, nutritionists, chiropractors, dentists, counselors— can use their healing abilities along with their professional expertise to help their clients. By touching, sending energy through the *focal center*, and *laying on of hands*, the professional can add his own natural ability to help the patient relax and receive full benefit of his care.

A veterinarian can hold a baby kitten during a routine examination and help it to relax or aid it in its healing process when it is faced with an infection or disease. When you are healing living things that cannot verbalize their feelings, keep in mind that a *healing* is not to be forced upon another being. Without cooperation of the other body, additional energy received will possibly disturb its balance and be rejected.

If you decide to heal your pet, trust your *gut response* for proper time and duration of the *healing* or follow the body signals your pet is sending you during the *healing*. If your cat tries to climb out of your arms to move away from you, do not persist with the *healing*. The animal is the best judge of timing and use of the healing energy. It is always wise, as a *psychic healer*, to have respect for the body you are healing to help maximize the effect of the energy you are transferring. If your cat remains with you, relaxing with your touch, chances are its body is responding positively to the *healing*.

A good friend can touch the shoulder or rub the hand of another during a time of trouble and transfer loving through healing energy to help him balance and face his problems.

Farmers, botanists, and horticulturists can, by touching the soil and plants they are growing, stimulate them to grow more healthy and productive with each touch. A horse breeder or owner of a kennel can raise heartier and healthier animals by touching and transferring healing energy to mothers and their offspring during and before delivery. Parents, sick children or loved ones in hospitals, or terminally ill family members at home or in hospices can be touched and healed at any time convenient, to promote healing and a sense of comfort to their bodies. An athlete, with a long training schedule to fulfill, having sustained an injury can facilitate recovery or gain a better sense of his body by establishing a healing schedule, especially during times of stress or competition.

Healing energy is universal. Used anywhere, anytime, with techniques that suit your natural ability, it enables you to lend a helping hand to yourself and others when energy is lów, imbalanced, or impeded. *Psychic healing* is not a cure but a means toward achieving and sustaining health, growth, and harmony.

Questions and Answers

What if I see colors change when I am doing aura healing? *What do I do?*

Since healing energy affects growth and change inside a person, he can begin to change while you are performing a *healing* on him. This change will be reflected in the person's *aura*. Depending on the colors perceived, you may continue healing in the same area or move your hands and focus to another area of the person's body. A person's *emotional aura* may change from a beige to dark red and then to a light shade of pink during a *healing*. The block you are affecting has been uncovered to show some possible underlying anger perpetuating the physical discomfort. During the *healing,* the anger is released and the body has begun its own healing of itself. If beige or red remains in the *aura* during the *healing,* you may choose to keep your hands on that particular area to advance the body's healing. Any information verbalized can shorten the duration of discomfort. Trust your *gut response* and information received to help you with the *healing*. Colors may change rapidly or not at all. The color change depends on the body's ability to recognize disruptions and heal itself, not upon your psychic ability.

141

How do I know if I am blocked when doing a healing? *What can I do to eliminate a block?*

If you sense a blocking of energy during or before a *healing* ask your body and/or *spirit* to help you in locating its source. If you are not sure about the energy flow or wish to double check your perceptions, your *gut response* and communication from your body and/or *spirit* will help you. Depending on the information and *gut response,* you can continue with the *healing* or try to eliminate your block to the healing energy. If you are having difficulty, reschedule the *healing* for a time when you feel more clear and are able to use your healing ability. The time between *healings* can be used to work with your body to eliminate blocks or problems that inhibit you. If you feel you can work with the healing energy, and push the block aside for the moment, continue with the *healing* and work on your problem after the *healing* is concluded.

Is it possible to find yourself sick from doing too many healings?

A *psychic healer* only contracts a sense of the illness to help him with healing. These symptoms can be released quickly as they are recognized. If a person has been healing people over an extended period of time, no cumulative effect from the *healings* will be experienced if he is actively working with both body and *spirit* and using all body channels and *preliminaries.* When you heal others frequently you receive the added benefit of healing energy over a long period of time. This helps to maintain a healthy body balance and harmonious flow of energy.

A *healer,* like any other person, can become sick when he ignores his body signals and his insights. If a *healer* avoids his own problems or continues to heal others when he is drained emotionally, or physically tired, his body balance will be affected. Additional *healings* when he is rested can help the *healer* to discover the cause of his own problems if he is willing to look.

Can you heal friends or relatives more easily than others?

A loving bond can add comfort and cooperation during a *healing*. Sharing and exchanging energy in a caring way adds to body harmony and balance. *Healing* a person who is close to you can also have its problems. If the *healer* is not comfortable with his healing ability, he may expect to heal the other person without including the person's own healing abilities. Basing his self worth on the outcome of the *healing* can create blocks due to tension or fear of failure. When both people share healing energy in a caring manner, without expectations other than promoting the healing process, the energy will be used to its best advantage.

Can a healer *transfer his or her own physical or emotional problems onto the person being healed?*

When working in an intimate situation such as a *healing*, a person can often transfer sensations of apprehension, nervousness, or depression onto another person. It is very important that the *healer release excess energy* before, during, and after a *healing* to avoid this possibility. It is also valuable to the *healer* to have good communication between his body and *spirit* so that any personal interference can be acknowledged and dealt with when it occurs.

Healing energy is universally shared and contains no blocks or problems. If the *healer's* own problems interfere with this energy, they can inhibit the energy flow to the other person. The problems remain for the *healer* to eliminate. When the blocks are removed, the energy can then flow into the other person and enable him to deal with his own blocks or problems.

eight

SPIRITS, GHOSTS, AND GUIDES

All living things, each attached to his own cloud, or *spirit*, share this energy nonphysically with one another. Some *spirits* remain in nonphysical form and are not attached to a body for learning. They learn and grow as energy in a nonphysical dimension. There is no difference between the energy of your *spirit* and the energy of these *spirits*, except the physical use of your body for your learning.

Remaining in *spirit* form is simply another way of growing. Because a *spirit* is not subject to physical density or time, it can grow in different ways, as a nonphysical energy pattern. When you die and leave your body, your energy rejoins your *spirit* and continues to develop nonphysically.

SPIRITS

Spirits without bodies can sometimes be seen or sensed as energy. Depending on their ability to condense their energies to physical limitations, they can sometimes appear as forms of light. When you see these *spirit lights* you are seeing or perceiving the *spirit's aura*. Nonphysical in origin, these colors are not generated by electricity or other physical factors. *Spirit lights* can sometimes be seen with the naked eye or sensed in the same way as when reading a person's *aura*.

Spirits can sometimes condense their energies and appear in body forms. They are not actually inhabiting physical bodies, but can create a sense of a physical form apparent to those who are able to use their psychic abilities to see or sense them. A *spirit* may effect a physical form when closely bonded to a physical person or place. For example, if you had a close bond with your grandmother, she may, after leaving her body at death, choose to remain nearer to your body to help you through your learning and growing. She may appear to you from time to time as a *spirit light*, in your dreams, or as a transparent physical form. Your *psychic* ability, used to perceive her, translates her energy into a visible body through your mind and physical senses. Since her body is not real it may appear to you as a filmlike image of herself. By allowing her *spirit* close to the physical plane her energy can be condensed into a form you can interpret.

If you were to reach out to touch your grandmother when you see her, you would be able to reach through her form and not be stopped by any body boundary. She is a *spirit* representing herself in a way that is comfortable for you to perceive. She no longer has or needs her physical body for her growing. Once accepted, this presence can be a comfort and an aid to you throughout your life.

A HAUNTING

When a *spirit* becomes attached to a physical person or place, or the physical person is continually focused on having their presence near them, the *spirit* moves away from its natural form of growing, as a nonphysical being. It then becomes encumbered by the physical plane, a plane which, without a body, it cannot use and experience fully. Because the *spirit* is in limbo, growing in a place for which it is least prepared, it can cause problems for the person it surrounds and for itself.

A *haunting* occurs when a person or persons who are in *spirit* form become bound to the physical level. Much sensationalism is associated with such *spirits* when they become attached to a place or house and refuse to leave it. When a *spirit* haunts a house, it either does not know it is only in energy form, having left its body quickly, or is unwilling to grow in the way that is best for it, the nonphysical dimension. Without a body restricting it, but conforming to some degree to density and physical matter, this *spirit* remains confused and unable to grow in its own dimension.

Since this *spirit* is focused physically, it is unable or unwilling to sense other *spirits* in energy form. Because it is without a physical body, it is unable to affect its physical environment. With its energy out of balance, it remains within the house causing disruption to the people it surrounds. It senses the house and is familiar with its energy, but not with the new inhabitants of the house. The *spirit* is not evil or negative; it is simply trying to remain in a form that no longer exists for it at present.

It is best for such *spirits* to leave their physical attachments and grow in the form best suited for them, as an energy pattern. If a *spirit* is constantly near a house, place, or person, even when the sole purpose is to counsel and help the individual, it is best for the *spirit* to work with the person or place on a nonphysical level. Having your grandmother work with your *spirit*, her energy can help you grow without disturbing your energy balance or inhibiting her own growth.

Not all *spirits* that manifest on the physical plane are in limbo or harmful to themselves. A *spirit* may, from time to time, manifest for you to relate more clearly to the information you are receiving from it, or to comfort you in time of loss. These *spirits* are then able to return to their natural way of growing and aid you on a nonphysical level of learning.

Whether visiting you briefly or attached to a house or physical area, such *spirits* are not pets or showpieces for neighbors and guests. They are people without bodies conveying a message, or blocked by their own confusion. They are not foreign to us since all energy is shared nonphysically.

To help those *spirits* in limbo, rather than perpetuate their confusion for your entertainment and stimulation, communicate with your own *spirit* to help them learn and find the best way to experience themselves. Your *spirit* can communicate with them on an energy level to facilitate their transition from a physical to a nonphysical state of being. When this is not possible, the use of a *medium* (see *Mediumship* Chapter) can help expedite the process. By communicating you have helped another eliminate disturbances that inhibit its ongoing development.

GHOSTS

Ghost stories, white sheets with black eyes, cartoons, and phrases like, "You look white as a ghost" or "You look like you've just seen a ghost," often are erroneous. Most people refer to *spirits* as *ghosts*. *Ghosts* are not whole states of energy. A *ghost* is a part of the energy of a *spirit* not a nonphysical being.

When a body dies, the energy within the body returns to its *spirit*. When a death occurs unexpectedly, as in cases of sudden fatal accidents, murder, suicide, or war, some of the *spirit's* energy during the transition from physical to nonphysical remains behind. This fragmented energy is referred to as a *ghost:* traces of the energy of the *spirit*.

Since these traces of energy are not the whole *spirit* energy, they do not contain a consciousness of the person. They do not house any body senses or conscious thought, nor do they carry any nonphysical perceptions or knowing. Like an arm that is severed in an accident while still moving, the muscles and nerves repeat the same movements without conscious thought. These *ghosts* of energy repeat movements of the energy left behind until they are dissipated by the movements or reabsorbed by the *spirit* now in nonphysical form.

A *ghost*, unlike a *spirit*, cannot communicate or take on a semblance of physical form. It simply repeats a movement. For example, if a person committed suicide by jumping out a window, the energy left behind may open the window repeatedly. It opens the window unconsciously as a reflexive act. *Ghosts* are mindless parts of energy that can be reabsorbed by the *spirit* to add to its energy form.

GUIDES

In physical life we become closer to certain people who partake in similar interests and attitudes. By sharing experiences we grow more intimate and love each other more deeply, strengthening our physical bonds.

Nonphysically we share experiences as well and grow

closer in energy with one another. As energy, we drift and merge together, helping to eliminate blocks that disturb our mutual and beneficial energy flow. *Spirits* that share these experiences more abundantly with us are our nonphysical friends. They are sometimes referred to as *guides, guardian angels,* or *spirits.*

Your *guide* or *guardian spirit* can help you on a physical level as well. Because you are in a body and sometimes limited by physical perceptions they, being nonphysical and not in a body, can help your *spirit* gain needed insight and energy to further your physical development. Friends, physical or nonphysical, can help you to discover things about yourself when you are too close to your own particular problem or your energy is confused. *Guides* can help you develop your psychic and creative abilities, adding their energy to your own *spirit's* energy when insight is needed or healing is generated. They can help you find direction in your life or even locate a pair of lost shoes or a needed parking place. They never take the place of your *spirit,* but, like good friends, help you achieve your potential.

Like our physical friendships, we have more than one *guide.* And, like a physical friend each *guide* complements and helps in areas best suited to it. As we grow each learns and teaches so that both *guide* and *spirit* gain from the experience.

A *guide* is, perhaps, the most enduring of all friends. On a nonphysical level, you have both shared experiences and energy beyond the physical limit of a lifetime. Since *guides* are old friends, their energies complement yours. Growing along with you, *guides* have your best interests at heart. And like good friends, they will not interfere with your perceptions, mistakes, and learnings. They are constant in their support and mutual sharing.

COMMUNICATING WITH YOUR GUIDES

Guides like other *spirits* can visit you in your dreams and help you in your waking state. As you learn, they continue to grow as well, adding to their own learnings. They remain in their nonphysical state, helping your *spirit* to grow at its own rate. Your *guides* are always close to you and available to help you.

Although not usually visible to us physically, we have as young children, sometimes seen or sensed the presence of our *guides*. Calling them *imaginary playmates,* we freely communicated with and accepted our *guides* in our everyday lives. We have, at times, even given them special names with which to identify them. As we became adults, possibly moving away from ourselves, we have also moved away from our communication with our *guides*.

If you have developed a continuous and reliable working relationship with your own body and *spirit,* you can again enjoy experiencing communication with your *guide(s)*. If you have not yet established a solid working relationship between your *spirit* and your body, to avoid confusion, it would be best to work with yourself and know your body and *spirit* before attempting any communication with your *guide(s)*. Before communicating with anyone else, it is always best to know and communicate with yourself.

When you begin to communicate with your *guide(s)*, it is important for you to be able to relax your body and *collect* your *energies* for focus. Just as you have experienced communication with your *spirit,* you can also enjoy communication with each *guide* that is close to you.

Exercise: Communicating with a Guide

For the purpose of this exercise you will find it easiest if you focus on communicating with one *guide*. After establishing communication, you can then communicate with any other *guides* available to you.

Practice *preliminaries*, and communicate with your body and your *spirit* so that they are working closely with you. If either your body or *spirit* has any reservations about the exercise, work with them until you feel satisfied that each is able to work with you.

Sense your *body center* for *gut response* and clear your mind of all thoughts.

Ask your *guide* a simple question: "Have I sensed you as a child before?" or "Have you ever come to me in my dreams?" A thought impression will appear inside your mind, similar to the way your *spirit* communicates with you. Your *guide's* "voice" will locate in a place inside your head other than where your body or *spirit* communicates. Experience the answer to your question by sensing it and locating its place inside your head.

Ask your *guide* another question, one that requires more than a simple yes or no answer. Clear your mind and allow the communication to enter your mind.

If you are confused during your body and *spirit* communication and cannot sense your *guide*, trust your *gut response* when receiving communication. It will verify what you are sensing. At first your *guide's* communication may seem exactly like the communication you receive from your *spirit*. As you continue to ask questions, you will gain a sense of your *guide* and the difference between your *guide's* energy and the energy and communication from your *spirit*.

If you are receiving no thoughts during communication, ask your body and/or your *spirit* to help you to allow your *guide's* energy to come closer to you for communication purposes. If you become frustrated, get busy doing some chore that is mindless, like emptying the garbage or washing the dishes, and ask your question again. Your own thoughts will be distracted and the energy will be allowed to flow smoothly from which to gain impressions. Trying hard to listen for communication sometimes produces the opposite effect and closes you off from your own ability of perceiving communication.

Once you have sensed and communicated with your *guide*, converse as often as you like with each other to gain a growing sense of one another. If you do not feel comfortable with your *guide's* energy, ask it to leave you for the moment. Open your body *channels* and ask your body and *spirit* to help you find the sense of your discomfort. Your *guide's* energy should always feel compatible to your own energy. When there is any problem or doubt about your *guide*, call upon your *spirit* to help you locate the discrepancy. Your *spirit* will also help you get used to the experience of communicating with another nonphysical being close to it.

A *guide* is a good friend and should be treated accordingly. If you wish to experience communication with other *guides*, let the guide with whom you have established a rapport assist you. Working with your *spirit* and your nonphysical guides can enable you to appreciate a wealth of friendship and sharing, not experienced through the visual eye.

Questions and Answers

If spirits can haunt us, should we be afraid of them? Can they do us physical harm?

A confused *spirit*, like a confused *person*, is not negative. Each is simply unable to see itself clearly. When a *spirit* or a person is confused each can disturb us if we let it. By extending ourselves to help such a person or *spirit*, we can alleviate the situation and allow each the opportunity to see the situation and itself realistically. Since we all share the same energy, it is not harmful to us. Working with your *spirit* and *guides* can help you deal with any problems of a nonphysical nature.

Is it easier to communicate with spirits *who appear in houses than with our* guides *or* spirits *we have known before?*

Since *guides* and *spirits* of loved ones share a strong bond with us, it is easier to communicate with them. A *spirit* confused about its state of existence will have a hard time communicating with you physically, because its own problems are inhibiting its energy flow. Once assuming its nonphysical state, it can then communicate openly with you if desired.

If I see blue or white spirit lights *can they change into the form of a person?*

Having a good working sense of your own body and *spirit* and sensing the energy of the *spirit* you can, by communicating with the *spirit,* ask it if it can effect a semblance of physical form. The spirit may or may not be able to do this, depending on its state of being and its reason for visiting the physical dimension. Whether you see or sense the *spirit* in body form is also dependent on the development of your own psychic ability. Simple communication with the *spirit* can allow you to sense and experience the spirit in whatever form you perceive it.

Can a ghost *remain on a physical level for a long period of time?*

Since a *ghost* is a part of a nonphysical energy pattern and serves no physical purpose, it will either be reabsorbed by the *spirit* or dispersed by its movements.

Why do we refer to spirits *as* ghosts?

The word *ghost* is a derivative of the word geist, meaning akin to *spirit*. The word *poltergeist*, meaning a bothersome *spirit*, has been shortened over the years to geist and misconstrued in its meaning. Thus, when referring to a *spirit*, benign or bothersome, we have used the word *ghost* in its place.

Can a guide take on a physical form so we can see it?

Depending on how able the *guide* is to affect the physical environment and how able we are to perceive it, a *guide* can appear as a *spirit* light or in physical form. *Guides* can also be perceived physically through dreams. If you are able to communicate with your *guide*, you might ask it to appear to you in a dream. Before retiring, also ask your body to remember in visual form the appearance of your *guide* in your dream.

Can a guide hurt or misguide you?

Like most friends, your *guide* is compatible and loving to you. Its energy, being close to your own, can be perceived. If your *guide* is blocked or its energy is imbalanced, it cannot help you in a clear and productive way. Using your *spirit* communication and your own *gut response*, you will be able to tell when this occurs. By recognizing an imbalance in your *guide's* energy you can, if your *guide* is willing, help it to rebalance and release its confusion. It is your choice to follow or not follow any friendly advice given at any time. By working with yourself and your *guide* in an open and honest atmosphere, you will both gain from the mutual experience.

Can a guide work with more than one physical person?

A *guide* can work with others on a nonphysical level as it grows. Like any friend, it will have contact and nonphysical relationships with other *spirits*. When helping a *spirit* and its energy on a physical level, a *guide* usually works

Spirits, Ghosts, and Guides

with only one person. If that person wishes the *guide* to help another person in a situation, it is the *guide's* own decision to do so. A good friend always has time and focus for the person closest to him, regardless of other bonds. Because your *guide* is a very close and dear friend, its energy and focus is primarily available to you.

nine

CLAIRVOYANCE

When you see *spirits, spirit lights,* shapes, faces, situations, colors, or symbols that are not physically visible to the naked eye, you are using *clairvoyance.* It is the ability to see or sense nonphysical energy or information in visual images. One can also use *clairvoyance* to see people and places that are not physically present. For example, using your *clairvoyant* ability, you can sit comfortably in New York and describe a house and its interior outside of San Francisco. This practice is called *remote viewing* and can be used to locate and describe physical phenomena from a distance.

At different times in your daily life you have experiences in *clairvoyance:* While you are walking down the street the face comes to mind of a friend who resembles the person moving toward you. Instead of this being merely a case of mistaken identity, your friend may call or meet with you soon after the occurrence. Faces or images may appear to you inside your forehead just before you fall asleep, or you may remember pictures of situations after awakening from a dream. These are natural extensions of *clairvoyant* abilities.

A person who has practiced using *clairvoyance*, a *clairvoyant*, can see or sense these visual images at will in a waking state. Whether you see images in your dreams or recognize them visually when you are awake, they are not creations of your mind. They are psychic impressions translated into visible picture for you to use daily to help give you insight and understanding about yourself and those around you.

Being *clairvoyant* is being forewarned. It affords you the opportunity to "tune in" to situations that may possibly occur in your life. These images are not tangible, but are representations of possibilities or information to be used for reference. The images and information are separate from your own thinking and feeling. You can receive them visually and work with them as learning tools.

VISIONS

Visions are a common form of *clairvoyance* used in many societies and religious rituals. People dance, chant, sing, or travel to special sacred places to receive *visions* that help them guide their lives. *Visions* are usually strong impressions, more vivid and clear than natural sight. They can be seen with eyes opened or closed and can include premonitions, events yet to come, symbols, numbers, faces, places, *guides*, and other *spirits*.

A *vision* usually lasts for a short period of time and is complete unto itself. A *vision* may or may not repeat itself, depending on the importance of the message or the ability of the *clairvoyant*. By trusting your *gut response* and allowing information to accompany what you are seeing, a *vision* can become a viable way of perceiving what you may not physically see or understand. Although usually related to future possibilities, *visions* can depict past and present concerns.

Clairvoyance can be incorporated in any type of *reading*. In *aura readings*, symbols and pictures may accompany the colors you are seeing. You may be able to see colors in an *aura* more vividly by using your *clairvoyant* ability. A *clairvoyant* can see *spirits*, loved ones, and guides, which will add to information given during a *psychic reading*, *psychometry reading*, or *psychic healing*. A *clairvoyant reading*, when used alone, focuses on visual images and incorporates information and impressions concerning them to the recipient.

There are several ways to practice your *clairvoyant* ability. By communicating with your body and *spirit* you can allow *visions* and images received in dreams to be remembered upon awakening. Communicating with your *guide* beforehand will also help you to gain a visual impression of it through your dreams. When awake, practice, with the aid of your body and *spirit*, exploring your process of *remote viewing*, to see and describe places that are distant from you. The more open you are to your *clairvoyant* ability, the more images you will allow through to you.

If you are unsure about how to proceed with developing your *clairvoyant* abilities, the following exercises will help you.

Exercise: Clairvoyance with Physical Objects

This exercise needs two or more people to be experienced fully.

One person should be selected to be the facilitator for the exercise. That person should have a tray or flat board and five small objects of varying shapes and sizes.

Place the objects in line, separate from each other, from left to right upon the tray. No two objects should be the same or similar, for example: A book, candle, cup, fork, bottle, and glove, make an acceptable combination.

The tray with the objects is to be placed before the *clairvoyants* so that they can study them.

Each *clairvoyant* should have a piece of paper and pencil beside him. If a *clairvoyant* wishes, he may write down a list of the objects at the top of the page for reference.

The facilitator should then remove the tray and objects from sight, and rearrange their order without indicating it to the *clairvoyants*. Leaving the tray and objects outside the room, the facilitator should clear his mind and return to the room.

All *clairvoyants* should practice *preliminaries*, communicate with their bodies, *spirits*, and *guides*, if desired, open *release channels* and *focal centers* and clear their minds.

When ready, each *clairvoyant* should write down the name of each object in order seen or sensed from left to right upon the tray.

When all are finished, the facilitator should return with the tray and objects as they were last arranged.

Check results. Communicate with your body or *spirit* when you are blocking or confused. If during the exercise you find yourself seeing or sensing an object in one place and then changing your impression, use your *gut response* to validate your perceptions and avoid confusion.

This exercise can be repeated many times. Each time the facilitator removes the tray from the room, the objects should be rearranged for the exercise to be practiced productively.

Before attempting each variation, the *clairvoyants* should *release excess energy* and clear their minds of all thoughts or images. Accumulated results from the continued exercise can be compared to see if you are using your *clairvoyant* ability beneficially.

Each person can take a turn at being the facilitator so that all members of the group experience using their *clairvoyant* abilities. The more times the exercise is repeated, the more chance you have to experience your *clairvoyant* ability and develop it.

Some people will have more tangible results than others. Others will need more time and experience to develop their *clairvoyant* abilities. This exercise is a physical way of opening yourself to your abilities, not of proving or testing them. If you are receiving limited results, devise other similar exercises with which to explore your abilities.

If you find yourself pushing for results rather than focusing on gaining experience in using *clairvoyance*, you will be able to discover how you hinder yourself and close yourself off from your natural psychic abilities. This in itself can be valuable in freeing you from blocks that disturb you when developing all other psychic abilities as well.

Exercise: Clairvoyance with One Object

Another exercise to practice uses the same tray and objects.

As before, select one facilitator and place pencils and paper before each clairvoyant. List the objects on the tray on top of the paper for reference.

Have the facilitator remove the tray with its objects. While the tray is out of view, the facilitator may choose only one object to remain on the tray and place it in the middle of the tray. All other objects should be placed in a bag to camouflage them. The facilitator should return to the room with the objects, leaving the object and tray behind. The facilitator can then place the bag out of sight and clear his mind.

All *clairvoyants* should practice *preliminaries*, communicate with their bodies, *spirits,* and *guides,* if desired, open *release channels* and *focal centers,* and clear their minds.

When ready, each *clairvoyant* should focus on the tray and write down the identity of the object seen or sensed.

When all are finished, the facilitator can retrieve the tray with the object on it and show it to the group to compare results.

This exercise can be repeated, changing facilitators from time to time. Before each object is focused on by the *clair-voyants,* each clairvoyant should clear his mind to allow images to be clearly seen or sensed.

SCRYING

Scrying is a *clairvoyant* method of seeing images and relating information about them. Used throughout the ages in many cultures, *scrying* involves a transparent surface, like a *crystal ball,* to focus upon. The *crystal ball,* a round, clear, glass-like ball, is placed upon a solid blank surface so that when one looks into it, images can be seen without distortion or interference. These images, seen clairvoyantly, can then be related to the person with the addition of any information received.

Scrying evokes memories of mystical men and women, gypsies, and carnival fortune tellers. It can be achieved without pageantry, costume, or mystery. Any transparent surface, such as water, can be used in place of a *crystal ball.* Scrying can be used anywhere and anytime as long as a transparent surface and skilled *clairvoyant* are present.

Exercise: Scrying

This exercise involves two or more people.

Each person should have a cup or glass, preferably untouched by others, before him. Any type of vessel will do, including a paper cup.

Partners should be chosen for *clairvoyant readings* and should situate themselves near each other in comfortable positions.

Decide which partner is to give the first *clairvoyant reading*. The person who is *reading* first can put his cup of water to the side, for the moment.

Place the cup of the person to be read in front of the *clairvoyant*.

Before beginning, each person should practice *preliminaries*, communicate with their bodies, and *spirits*, and *guides*, if desired, and open *release channels* and *focal centers*.

While the *clairvoyant* is clearing his mind, the person being read should place both hands comfortably around his cup to allow his energy to flow into the water. The water will then serve as a contact to his energy from which the *clairvoyant* can gain impressions. This need not be done when *scrying* with a *crystal ball*, because the *crystal ball* itself is usually untouched by human hands. Touching the cup ensures the *clairvoyant* that additional energy will not intrude on the *reading*.

When both people are ready, the person being read can remove his hands from the cup.

The *clairvoyant*, with mind cleared, can now gaze into the water and allow his eyes to become unfocused as in *aura reading*. The water is a focal point for images and can be studied for the full *reading* or glanced at from time to time, depending on what is comfortable for the clairvoyant.

As the *clairvoyant* gazes into the water, he may see or sense shapes, forms, objects, colors, people, symbols or situations in the water or in his mind. By experimenting, the *reader* will find the best way to receive visual impressions. Some people will physically see symbols in the cup or water, others will see them only in their minds, usually on the inside of their foreheads. When reading clairvoyantly, some people will only sense images inside their heads. Others will sense and see these images. Whatever you perceive, verbalize all impressions and images to the other person. Any further insights that come to you about these images should also be expressed. Do not stop yourself when you first see an image but allow any and all information coming to you to be verbalized.

When you reach a stopping point, relax, clear your mind, and gaze into the water again.

When there are no further images or impressions coming forth the *clairvoyant reading* is concluded.

Release all *excess energy* into an inanimate object and through your *release channel.*

If you are unsure of information or images or are blocking yourself from your *clairvoyant* ability, use your *gut response* to help you locate any problems. If, at any time during the *reading,* you sense or see an image you wish to clarify, ask your body and your *spirit* to help you focus more clearly.

After the *reading* is finished, place the cup aside. The *clairvoyant* should now place his cup of water before the other person.

The new *clairvoyant reading* should follow all procedures described previously so that both partners experience reading and being read.

This exercise can be repeated using different partners to gain a continued sense of using *clairvoyance.*

Exercise: Scrying for Yourself

An additional exercise can be used when one wants to gain *clairvoyant* impressions for himself.

Follow the same procedure described in *scrying,* using and then touching your own cup of water or *crystal ball.*

When reading for yourself be sure to enlist the help of your *gut response,* body, and *spirit* for verification of information received. If you find yourself tensing or trying too hard to see images, *release excess energy* into an inanimate object before retouching the cup again. Clear your mind and allow your eyes to become unfocused as they stare into the water or *crystal ball.* Look away from time to time then return to focus if you become distracted during your own *reading.*

With practice, you will be able to focus more readily, and soon be able to perceive images and information without use of any physical tool except your own body.

DAILY USES FOR CLAIRVOYANCE

Clairvoyance can be used in many ways in your daily life. If you have lost an object and want to locate it without physical effort, practice *preliminaries,* clear your mind, and focus on the object to see or sense where it is situated. Allow visual perceptions or information into your mind and follow them, using your *gut response* as your barometer to lead you to the object.

Clairvoyance is used effectively to solve crimes and reconstruct various acts that are without witnesses. A *clairvoyant,* having minimal information about the person or crime, can visualize the place of the crime, the person committing the crime, or the actual reenactment of the crime itself.

Since *clairvoyant* ability is nonphysically oriented, it can be used to see into the past, present, and future at any given time. By using a description of a car, highway sign, or area, a *clairvoyant* can be helpful in solving robberies and finding buried stolen goods when no verifiable information is known.

Clairvoyance can be a comfort when you focus on a person you love who is in the hospital, away on business, or living a distance from you. By *remote viewing* of loved ones, you can see how they are and bring their images closer to you.

When driving a car or using any machinery you can avoid accidents, including airplane crashes, by using your *clairvoyant* ability to see things before they happen. With practice, your *clairvoyant* ability can be an asset in your life, enabling you to function smoothly without incident.

Clairvoyance is used to find buried treasure, locate oil and other natural resources, and uncover important documents and heirlooms left behind by a deceased relative. *Clairvoyance* can even be used to find your child at the beach, when he has wandered away from you, or quickly discover bargain specials in the supermarket or department store. *Clairvoyance* can even be used to avoid the encounter of an awkward and uneventful blind date.

Using *clairvoyance* enables you to see what to prepare for, whether it be a sudden confrontation, a protective move to avoid an accident, or where to find the extra sweater you misplaced on your vacation. It can help you foresee natural disasters, snowstorms, sunny days, when the dentist is in his office for you to return his call, or which lane of traffic on the bridge will be free for your homeward journey.

You will find that your *clairvoyant* ability, used by itself or in conjunction with your other psychic abilities, will help you enhance your perceptions of your own life and the lives of those around you. The images you see will become more clear to you as you practice and the information given will expand upon what you are seeing. The more you use your *clairvoyant* ability, the more you will realize that things do not always appear as they seem.

Questions and Answers

Are guides clairvoyant?

Since *clairvoyance* is a nonphysical ability and *guides* exist in the nonphysical dimension, it is their natural way of seeing and sensing, especially when working with the physical environment. Your *guide* can help you develop your own *clairvoyant* ability. When working with your *spirit,* your *guide* can assist your *spirit* by sharing its own perceptions and helping to transfer them to your body.

If you are blind or have a vision impairment, can it affect your clairvoyant *ability?*

Physical limitations do not influence your psychic abilities. They sometimes encourage you to rely on them in place of physical sight. A blind or vision-impaired person can sense or perceive visual impressions more clearly than those with sight, because he may be more experienced and practiced in using his *clairvoyant* abilities. A person blind from birth may have some difficulties relating what he is seeing or sensing in physical terms because of lack of experience at seeing what is physical. An impairment of the body will not hamper psychic abilities unless the impairment blocks or disturbs the person's energy flow.

What if I see something in a vision *or dream and it doesn't happen? Is it wrong?*

You may, at first, not be perceiving or interpreting your *vision* or dream accurately. Your *gut response* and body and *spirit* communication will aid in gaining verifiable results. You may have seen something that has already happened or a symbolic representation of the occurrence. Again, your *gut response* and communication will help you understand what you are seeing. For example, you may see a child close to you and think the information means you are going to have a baby. The child may actually be a symbol representing yourself relating to a situation in which you have acted immaturely, or the child may be an image to remind you to be true to yourself and trust your childlike qualities hidden behind your defenses. By allowing information that follows to be verbalized, you can sort through images and find meanings relevant to them.

There will be times when you will receive an image or *vision* that will not happen for a long time or may not come to pass, because you will have grown and changed between the time of the *vision* and its actual happening. Your *gut response* and additional information about the *vision* or image will help you place it in perspective within your life.

Instead of seeing clairvoyantly, *can my mind be replaying images I have already seen and not noticed from some other time in my life?*

When you are unused to using your *clairvoyant* ability you can confuse these nonphysical perceptions with pictures your mind remembers. When beginning to use your *clairvoyant* ability, be sure to practice *preliminaries*, communicate with your body and *spirit*, and clear your mind before each experience if possible. If you are confused as to the derivation of images seen, simply ask your *gut* to respond or communicate with your body to alleviate the distractions. Both will help you to verify what you are seeing *clairvoyantly* and what are accumulated mental images. Once this is defined, your body can eliminate through your *release channel* any excess energy and images not needed for your growing. Those images remaining may be useful to you and can be expanded upon by using your *clairvoyant* ability.

Can I see my guide or loved ones, or even my own spirit, clairvoyantly?

Since *clairvoyance* is nonphysical sight, you can see or sense anyone in nonphysical form, including your own *spirit*. This is often done when you are sleeping, in dreams. With practice you can visualize a physical representation of your *guide*, loved one, or self. *Clairvoyance* can be used to visualize physically and nonphysically, because the energy used is limited only by your own perceptions of it.

ten

MEDIUMSHIP

If we can see and read nonphysical energy, we can also communicate with those in energy form. *Mediumship* is the ability to communicate nonphysically. When you listen and speak with your *spirit* or your *guide*, you are using your *mediumistic* ability.

People who practice *mediumship* are called *mediums* or *sensitives*. They are go-betweens, corresponding with physical and nonphysical energy. A *sensitive* or *medium* is finely tuned to all of the energy around him. Like an antenna, his body is reactive to both physical and nonphysical energy.

A *sensitive* or *medium* may find himself near or around a person who is sad or upset and feel a sensation of that distress. A *medium* may also sense an impending dangerous situation before it happens or before others realize it exists. A *medium* or *sensitive* may also sense the presence of a loved one, in spirit form, near or around another person while that person does not sense it.

A *medium* is not a helpless victim of this energy. Once aware of this psychic ability, the *medium* can expel any disturbance sensed the same way a *psychic healer* does when relieving himself of excess physical symptoms during a *healing*. The energy sensed can add insight and help with daily encounters and activities. A medium can readily sense and communicate nonphysically with other *spirits* for insight about himself, and enjoy the added benefit of sharing and communicating with *spirit* friends and physical friends who cannot communicate verbally. A *medium* can receive information from a *spirit*, know when an animal needs nurturing, if a child wants to be left alone, and how a plant is reacting to its new environment.

Many people are *sensitives* or *mediums* and do not realize it. Because their reactions have no tangible derivation, they go through their days constantly reacting to the energy around them, thinking it is theirs. A person riding a bus may become angry for no obvious reason. As the ride continues his anger progresses. The person seated in front of him had just had a fight with his neighbor and is harboring his angry feelings. The *sensitive,* unaware of his *mediumistic* ability, holds onto this anger for the rest of the morning until the energy naturally dissipates. Some *mediums* take on this energy, thinking it their own, and absorb it in their bodies. This disturbs their energy balance and disrupts the flow of their daily activities.

Receiving energy is not dangerous. When the energy is not your own, it will dissipate with time. Being aware of your *mediumistic* ability, you can easily eliminate any excess energy through your *release channel* and continue through your day without disruption. Being a *medium* does not mean that you will only react to disruptive energy. A *sensitive* may walk to work feeling unduly excited and happy. Upon starting business he may receive a phone call filled with good news or find he has a chance to advance to the position he was seeking in the firm. Your *mediumistic* ability can protect and alert you to possible interference and also be fruitful for gaining insight and enjoyment in living.

You will find, with practice, that if you are talking to a person or entering a situation and begin to feel a headache, anxiety, elation, depression, or a combination of feelings for no tangible reason, you will be able to separate these feelings from yourself and eliminate them. Left with insight about the reaction, you can then deal with the person or situation in a suitable way. Whenever you are in doubt, simply communicate with your body and *spirit*, trust your *gut response* to the reaction, and eliminate all excess energy through your *release channel*. Those feelings that remain are your own and will enable you to learn more about yourself and your defenses in the situation. Rather than feeling blindly victimized by the moment you will be able to use it, along with your *mediumistic* ability, to your advantage.

Mediumship, when used for the purpose of communication with *spirits,* can be practiced in several ways. Each type of *mediumship* is consistent with the *medium's* ability to communicate and his body comfort.

INDIRECT VOICE COMMUNICATION

Indirect voice communication occurs when a *medium* senses the energy of a *spirit* and translates these impressions verbally. In the course of a *reading* of this type, the *medium* can read a *spirit* just as you might read another physical person during a *psychic reading. Indirect voice communication* is incorporated in a *psychic reading* when the person for whom you are reading wishes information from a *guide,* loved one, or other *spirit,* including his own. The information relayed is received as impressions and verbalized by the *medium*.

If the *medium* is inexperienced he may allow his own feelings or thoughts to interfere with such a communication, or if more than one *spirit* is communicating, the *medium* may confuse the information received. With practice, the *medium* will be able to relay all information received from the *spirit(s)* present during the *indirect voice communication*.

DIRECT VOICE COMMUNICATION

In *direct voice communication*, the *medium* relates the information received from a *spirit*, word for word, as it is communicated. The *medium* repeats each word separately as it comes into his mind from the *spirit* communicating. The difference between *direct voice communication* and *indirect voice communication* can be related to a telephone conversation. If a friend is hearing the conversation and relating it to you from the source on the other end of the receiver you are experiencing *indirect voice communication*. If you are holding the receiver and hearing the words exactly as they are spoken, you are experiencing *direct voice communication*.

When using *indirect voice communication* or *direct voice communication*, the *spirits(s)* communicating can be sensed and described to the other person by the *medium*.

Direct voice communication can be incorporated within a *psychic reading* or any other type of *reading* when communication from a *spirit(s)* is desired. When using *direct voice communication*, since you are dealing directly with the exact words transmitted, there is less confusion during a communication if more than one *spirit* is present. *Direct voice communication* can be the entire focus of a *reading* for another person. Such a *reading* is called a *mediumistic reading*.

In a *mediumistic reading*, the *medium* using *direct voice communication* may be conscious or unconscious during the transference of information from a *spirit*. This unconscious state used for communication purposes is called a *trance*. In a *trance*, the body of the *medium* is either shared by a *spirit* other than its own during the communication or the *medium's spirit* leaves its body and is replaced by the *communicating spirit* during the *mediumistic reading*.

SEMI-TRANCE COMMUNICATION

Semi-trance communication occurs when the *medium*, with full cooperation from his body and his *spirit*, allows another *spirit* to enter his body and share it with his own *spirit* for the time of the communication. It is most important for the *medium* to be able to communicate openly with his own body and *spirit* so that the transition and communication will be productive for the *medium* and the person for whom he is reading.

What physically happens when a *medium* goes into *semi-trance?*

The *medium* situates his body in a supported and comfortable position, usually in a durable chair or in a reclining position. With the help of the *medium's guides* and his own body and *spirit*, the *communicating spirit* enters the body. As the *communicating spirit* enters the body, the *medium's* own *spirit* recedes and compresses its energy somewhere inside the body to allow space for the energy of the *communicating spirit*. The *medium's spirit* can locate itself near the spinal column or *body center* to allow the *communicating spirit* full access to the body's physical apparatus for communication.

With the help of the *medium's* body, the *communicating spirit* can use its mind, vocal cords, arms, face, and lungs during the communication. The *communicating spirit* shares the *medium's* body to communicate with because it does not have a body of its own. The *medium's spirit* remains in its compressed state inside its body throughout the communication and is aware of all that is being transmitted.

When communication is completed, the *communicating spirit*, with the help of the body and its *guides*, leaves the *medium's* body and rejoins its own nonphysical energy. The *medium's spirit* expands its energy inside the body and fills the body as the energy of the *communicating spirit* leaves. When the *communicating spirit* is gone, the body of the *medium* returns to its normal functions.

The time limit for a *semi-trance communication* is dependent on the amount of information to be given and the comfort of both the *communicating spirit* and the *medium's* body and *spirit* during communication. During a *semi-trance reading*, if the *medium* is willing, more than one *spirit* can communicate, each entering, sharing the body, communicating, and then leaving the body. All communications are separate and dependent on the mutual agreement of the *medium* and *communicating spirit(s)*.

Any excessive energy retained in the body can then be released by the *medium* into an inanimate object and through his *release channel*.

FULL-TRANCE COMMUNICATION

Full-trance communication is slightly different from *semi-trance communication*. *Full-trance* is very similar to a sleep state we experience when we leave our bodies at night to experience our nonphysical energy. In *full-trance communication*, the *medium's spirit* consciously leaves the *medi-*

um's body during the communication. When you *astral project* during sleep, some of your energy remains in your body, but another *spirit* does not enter it.

In *full-trance communication,* the *medium's* body is also situated in a well-supported position, reclined or seated. Relaxing his body, the *medium* communicates with his body, *spirit,* and *guides* to gain needed cooperation for the *full-trance communication.*

When ready, the *medium's spirit* leaves its body, assisted by its *guides,* and the *communicating spirit* enters the body and fills it with its energy. It uses the body's mind and vocal cords as well as any other body parts for the communication. The *medium's spirit,* still attached to its body at the *energy exchange channel,* may remain near the body or reunite with the rest of its energy on a nonphysical level.

Throughout the communication, the *communicating spirit* remains in the body using it to verbalize information given. When the communication is concluded, the body assists the *communicating spirit,* with the help of *guides,* to leave and rejoin its energy on a nonphysical level. When the *communicating spirit* has left, the *medium's* own *spirit* returns filling the body with its energy as before.

The time limit for a *full-trance communication* is dependent on the *medium,* his body and *spirit,* and the *communicating spirit.* If more than one *spirit* wishes to communicate through the body during *full-trance communication,* the second *communicating spirit* enters the body, with the help of *guides,* after the first *communicating spirit* leaves. When all communication is finished, the *medium's spirit* returns to full use of its body.

Some *spirits,* not having had bodies of their own, may be unused to working inside a body to give communication. With practice, an experienced *medium* can work with *guides* and *communicating spirits* to facilitate communication in this manner.

When witnessing a *medium* giving *semi-trance* or *full-trance communication*, you may find that the presence of another *spirit* inside the body alters vocal range, language, facial features, and body movements, depending on the experience of the *communicating spirit's* use of a body. If you are a *sensitive* or *medium* watching a *mediumistic reading*, your added ability will help you to sense the differences between *communicating spirits* and the transition of *spirits* leaving and entering the body of the *medium*.

There are advantages and disadvantages when using *semi-trance* or *full-trance communication*. In *semi-trance communication*, one can experience his own body from a different perspective inside the body. By sensing the entry and departure of the *communicating spirit* while in the body, your *spirit* can recognize ways in which you hinder yourself when you *astral project* while sleeping. When using *semi-trance communication*, you have the added aspect of your *spirit* remaining within your body during the communication should any problems arise for the *communicating spirit* during communication, or when leaving the body.

In *full-trance communication*, you can experience full *astral projection* and the nonphysical level of being. Other *communicating spirits* can learn more about physical bodies by sharing yours, and your *spirit* can bring back impressions to your body from its nonphysical self. *Full-trance* also enables you to bring extra healing energy inside your body from another *spirit*, or to gain insight from another source firsthand about body problems you may be having.

In both *semi-trance* and *full-trance communication*, *guides* can be very helpful with sensing problems and other *spirits*, and easing the process of transition before and after communication. A *guide* also can enter a *medium's* body for communication purposes or to help discover difficulties with energy flow inside the *medium's* body. Since a *guide's* energy is most compatible with the *spirit* it is assisting, the transition before, during, and after communication will be a pleasant one.

To communicate *mediumistically*, one must always maintain a close and constant communication and relationship with both body and *spirit*. *Mediumistic communication* should not be attempted without establishing and continuing this strong communication. The added experience of *astral projection* while conscious also is helpful. To begin *semi-trance* or *full-trance communication* using your *mediumistic* ability, an experienced and knowledgeable *medium* should always be present to assist you with any problems that might arise.

Working cooperatively with your body and *spirit*, and *guides*, *mediumship* can be a beautiful and enlightening venture. It is the closest conscious experience we have to being nonphysical after we leave our bodies at death. The existing difference between the two is that, in *mediumship*, the *spirit* returns to the body, allowing it to function and continue with its life in an enriched and enlivened way.

What happens when problems arise during a *mediumistic* communication? What if the *medium's* body is unwilling to cooperate? What if the *medium's spirit* or the *communicating spirit* refuses to help the communication?

If the body of the *medium* blocks the *communicating spirit*, or is uncooperative during the communication, the communication cannot be achieved. If the *medium's spirit* refuses to work with the body, or the *communicating spirit* is not cooperative, then there is a lack of fluidity and control during the communication. When the *medium* allows another *spirit* inside his body without the full cooperation of his body and *spirit* or the *communicating spirit*, serious problems can arise.

POSSESSION

Numerous frightening movies and countless spine chilling stories have been told about *possessions*. The media have substituted terror and fear for information about such events. *Possessions* are not common and occur only in isolated instances. When they do happen, they can be rectified easily with the help of an experienced *medium*.

Imagine a body whose *spirit* refuses to work with it and constantly distances its consciousness from the physical body. Although this *spirit* still is attached to the body, helping it with its basic functions, it remains a passive participant in the person's physical development and learning.

When another *spirit* has left its own body suddenly, due to a suicide, fatal accident, or act of war, it remains attached to the physical environment. In its confusion, it blocks itself from its own nonphysical energy state. When a body, whose *spirit* is divorced from it, happens by, the confused spirit mistakes it for its own body, since both bodies are empty of conscious nonphysical energy, and enters it. The confused *spirit* may also, in its search for its own body, enter the body of the divorced *spirit* to use it for help and communicating purposes. Without the aid of the body's own *spirit*, the confused *spirit* assumes control and fills the body with its energy.

The body, unprepared for this confused energy, reacts and struggles to force this unfamiliar energy out. Without the help of the body's own *spirit*, this struggle can extend over a period of time. When an unfamiliar *spirit* inhabits a body against its will, it is called a *possession*.

Another *spirit* can possess only a body whose *spirit* is divorced from it and refuses to cooperate with it. If the body's own *spirit* abandoned it totally, the body would die. Since the body is attached still to its *spirit* via the *energy exchange channel,* it remains alive, but it cannot participate fully with its own nonphysical energy. This energy is consciously replaced by the confused spirit that possesses it.

SEMI-POSSESSION

If a confused *spirit* enters another body and leaves it from time to time, the person experiences a *semi-possession.* In *semi-possession,* the body may force the confused *spirit* from itself intermittently as it struggles for control, or the confused *spirit* may enter it when the body's own *spirit* leaves it and then remove itself when the body's *spirit* returns.

Although the confused *spirit* does not always remain within the body, it does, when inside it, use its nonphysical consciousness to direct body movement. The body *semi-possessed* by another *spirit* may feel balanced then imbalanced, from time to time, as both *spirits* exchange use of the body.

FULL POSSESSION

When the confused *spirit* remains inside the body and does not leave it while the body's own *spirit* stays outside of the body, it is called *full possession.* During *full possession,* the confused *spirit* assumes full use of the body and leads it to situations and people familiar with it.

The *spirit* assuming control over the body during *semi-possession* or *full possession* is not negative or evil. It is confused and mistaken and usually imbalanced. The confused *spirit* does not necessarily want to harm or intrude upon the body. It knows no other way of being, because it is blocked from its reality and perceptions. If a person barged into your house and, in his confused state, assumed it was his house, you would be disturbed and your life would be upset. You would, to alleviate the situation, try to force him out, ask for help, or try to communicate and reason with him. When such a thing occurs between a body and a confused *spirit,* the process is the same.

EXORCISM

A simple process to restore the body to its natural balance and harmony is called an *exorcism.* Although usually depicted as a religious ceremony involving evil and bizarre, even lethal, behavior, an *exorcism* is a realistic way of dealing with an unfortunate situation. A skilled *medium* can perform an *exorcism* by communicating with the confused *spirit* and transferring energy to the *possessed* body to help the confused *spirit* leave.

Exorcisms have been known and used throughout history to restore balance and facilitate body and spirit harmony. Many cultures incorporate religious ceremony and ritual with an *exorcism.* In psychic terms, an *exorcism* involves communication with all *spirits* involved and assistance in reestablishing basic self harmony.

What actually occurs during an *exorcism?*

When a confused *spirit* is in *full possession* of a person's body, a *medium* is consulted to perform an *exorcism.* If the confused *spirit* enters and leaves the body at will, as in a *semi-possession,* the *medium* must wait until the confused *spirit* enters the body again or transfers energy to the body, as when giving a *psychic healing,* so as to draw the confused *spirit* back inside the body, in order to perform the *exorcism.*

Before beginning an *exorcism,* the *medium* communicates with his body and *spirit* and *guides* to gain an open communication for help during the *exorcism*. The *medium* practices *preliminaries* and opens all body channels.

When ready, the *medium* talks to the confused *spirit* as it resides within the body of the possessed person. By communicating with the confused *spirit* in this way, the *medium* can sense the *spirit* and gain insight about it. The *medium*, having established contact with the confused *spirit*, places his hands upon the person's body, one hand on the *focal center*, the other on the *body center*, as in *basic healing*. The energy flows through the *medium* and adds to the confused *spirit's* energy inside the body to help balance and restore it to its natural state. By communicating with the *spirit* during this process, the *medium* can gain feedback from the *spirit* and help it to relax its energy and balance itself if additional problems arise. With the help of *guides* and its own nonphysical self, the *spirit* can then leave the body and rejoin itself on a nonphysical level.

The *medium* continues *laying on of hands* at both the *body* and *focal centers* during the transition and after the *spirit* leaves the body it has been possessing. The *medium* then communicates with the body's own spirit, helping it to understand and reassume cooperation with its body. Once in the body, the *medium* aids the body and *spirit*, so that communication and cooperation can continue. The body and *spirit* can then reassume learning and growing together, while the once confused *spirit*, now balanced, continues to develop on an energy level.

Possessions and *exorcisms*, although quite real, occur only in rare cases. With proper knowledge and skilled *mediumistic* ability, the situation can be rectified quickly. Only with full knowledge of body and *spirit* communication and *trance* techniques, should a person explore and practice his *mediumistic* abilities. With the help of a trained *medium*, the transition and experience can be a gratifying endeavor.

181

DAILY USES FOR MEDIUMSHIP

Mediumistic readings are a way of knowing, sensing, and communicating with those on the nonphysical level. A *medium* can allow the *spirit* of a loved one to communicate to its child, mate or friend to give them comfort and assurance of its wellbeing. A *spirit* can communicate the whereabouts of specific valuables or objects left behind after death. When *mediumistic readings* are given in a group setting it is called a *séance*. In a *séance*, one or more *mediums* are present within the group of people to give information and communication, from a *spirit* or *spirits*, to group members. Whether in a *séance* or private *reading*, *mediumistic* communication with *guides* and other *spirits* can help you gain a better perspective about yourself, your physical life, and those on a nonphysical level.

Mediumistic ability need not be far removed from daily life. It can be used to sense dangerous situations or people counterproductive to your life. Being a *sensitive* can help you enjoy positive instances and people more fully by experiencing them on all levels of being. *Healings* can be done *mediumistically* to aid in wellbeing and diagnose problems or physical disturbances of the body.

In most cultures, spiritual leaders, medicine men, and counsels are most respected for their use of *mediumistic communication* when healing or giving guidance. One of the most physically documented modern *healers* in the United States was Edgar Cayce, who gave *healings* and prescribed remedies while participating in *full-trance communication*.

Mediumship, used knowledgeably, can assist people nonphysically with problems they cannot resolve mentally; when their spirits are imbalanced, causing problems in daily life; when their houses are haunted or when disturbing people enter their lives. Being responsible both physically and nonphysically ensures a healthy and balanced way of growing. *Mediumistic* ability adds insightful dimension to this participation.

QUESTIONS AND ANSWERS

How can one recognize a possession?

When a body is possessed, behavior becomes very erratic and the body's personality changes dramatically. Not all people with multiple personalities are possessed. When a person is *possessed*, he may react quite physically by being angry and depressed, gain weight in large amounts, break out in rashes or become ill, and, when semi-possessed, cry out for help to alert others to the situation by acting out or verbalizing his frustration and confusion. If you are unsure about whether someone is possessed, bring the person or a photograph of the person to a skilled *medium* for confirmation.

How can someone who hasn't developed his mediumistic *ability conduct an* exorcism *if it is needed?*

If possible, elicit the help of a trained *medium* for the *exorcism*. When none are available to you, keep in mind that the confused *spirit* and the body of the possessed person is each uncomfortable and does not want to remain in this state. By communicating with your own body and *spirit* and *collecting* your own *energy*, you ensure focus and protection for yourself throughout the *exorcism*. Talk to the other person and allow them to communicate whatever impressions come into their mind from the confused *spirit*. By speaking kindly and encouraging the confused *spirit* to allow your energy in to balance it while you place your hands on the *body* and *focal centers*, you can help the confused *spirit* to rebalance its energy so it can leave the person's body and go on with its living. You can also help the person's body and his own *spirit* rejoin and live more productively.

How do I know I can trust myself to go into full-trance?

Ask your body this question. Then ask your *spirit* the same question. If both responses are positive and you feel you have a good working relationship between your body and your *spirit,* then ask a skilled *medium* to assist you in learning and experiencing the techniques used in *full-trance communication.*

Why would a spirit *want to remain in a body that doesn't want it?*

For that confused *spirit,* entering a body is like coming in out of a rainstorm. It has known being in a body and suddenly is without one. Relieved to have a physical vehicle, it is too confused to sense any differences. Too imbalanced to perceive nonphysical communication or sense itself on an energy level, it remains struggling with the body for control. When it is assisted in sensing its own energy and is rebalanced, it willingly seeks the level with which it is most comfortable, the nonphysical way of growing.

Is it possible to go into semi-trance *or* full-trance *while sleeping?*

Trance is a conscious means of communicating. *Semi-trance* or *full-trance communications* are decided upon before they occur. When sleeping, your body is at rest and would not be included in deciding or working with the process. Since *trance* work always is practiced with the full communication of body and *spirit,* the *communicating spirit* would not be allowed to enter the body and the body itself would not be conscious to work with the communication. Neither the body nor the *spirit* would benefit from a *mediumistic* communication while in the sleep state.

eleven

OUIJA BOARDS

A *ouija board* is not a toy; it is a *mediumistic* tool. *Ouija boards* have been used for centuries in Eastern cultures to communicate with *spirits* and to divine information. The *ouija board* is comprised of two essential parts: the *alphabet board* and the *planchette* that moves upon it.

THE ALPHABET BOARD

The *alphabet board* can be constructed from any durable material and must be flat enough for a *planchette* to rest and move atop it. An *alphabet board* can be made from wood, cardboard, or even a piece of paper. For the *alphabet board* to be functional, each letter of the alphabet should be written in order across the board surface. The letters should be spaced equidistant from each other and form two separate rows with a wide space between them. The language of the letters on the *alphabet board* is native to the *medium* who uses it.

In addition to the letters, numbers can be added to the surface of the board. All numbers listed from 0–9 should be spaced equidistant from each other in a line near the lower edge of the board. *Alphabet boards* can have pictures decorating them or the words YES or NO written in available corners. Only the alphabetical letters are necessary for the *ouija board* to function properly. Any additional information can be spelled out through them.

THE PLANCHETTE

The *planchette* is the heart of the *ouija board*. Without a *planchette*, communication cannot be established. The *planchette* is a small object through which the *spirit* communicates. In *semi-trance* or *full-trance communication*, the body of the *medium* is used for giving *spirit* communication. When using a *ouija board*, the *planchette* serves the same purpose as the *medium's* body during communication.

If a *ouija board* is not available, an experienced *medium* can use any surface and a comfortable flat object with which to communicate. Visualizing the letters upon a blank surface, the *medium* can use the object as a *planchette* to gain information. The design of the *planchette* does not need to be artistic, but it must be able to move easily across a flat surface without friction, and should be wide enough for two people to place their fingertips on it across from each other. It should also have a central point so that each letter can be seen and read for communication.

COMMUNICATING THROUGH
A OUIJA BOARD

A *spirit* may communicate through a *ouija board* for many reasons. It may wish to send a message to a loved one, impart insight and information, or gain a closer sense of the physical world.

The main difference between *ouija board communication* and *full* or *semi-trance communication* is that no *spirit* has grown with the *planchette* as your *spirit* has grown with your body. The *spirit* decides to use the *planchette* as a physical contact to learn more about the physical world or to impart information. This *spirit* is called a *control spirit*.

THE CONTROL SPIRIT

The *control spirit* assumes responsibility for the *planchette* in the same way that your *spirit* protects your body during communication. Its energy always remains attached to the *planchette* while other *spirits* communicate through it. This prevents the *medium* using the *ouija board* from being disturbed by confused *spirits* or miscommunication from several *spirits*.

The *control spirit*, similar to a body's spirit, decides which *spirit* will enter the *planchette* at any given time for the purpose of communication. All *spirits* are sensed and agreed upon by the *control spirit* and the *medium* using the *ouija board* before they are allowed to communicate through the *planchette*. There is no limit to the number of *spirits* with whom you can communicate through a *ouija board*. Upon agreement, the *control spirit* allows each, in turn, to communicate its information.

The *control spirit* is chosen by either your *guide(s)* or your own *spirit* on a nonphysical level. If you have a *ouija board,* ask your *guide* or *spirit* to help you select a *control spirit.* Both *guides* and your *spirit* have your best interests known to them and will ask a *spirit* wishing to communicate with you and experience the physical level to become the *control spirit* for your *ouija board.* It is always a mutual agreement among the *guide,* the spirit wanting to communicate, and the *medium* himself. Your *spirit* and *guide* will be sure to explain the responsibility of being a *control spirit* to the communicating *spirit* and will find a strong communicator for you.

In rare instances, *guides* can be *control spirits* on a *ouija board.* This is done when a *guide* decides to maintain a close physical contact with the person whom it is helping. Usually your *guide* does not use a *ouija board* as a *control spirit,* because this limits its flexibility to communicate with and help you at any given time. Limited to the physical contact, it must wait for the intervals when you use the *ouija board* for communication rather than communicate with your *spirit* or body whenever it is needed. Your *guides* can, if necessary, use the *ouija board* with the help of the *control spirit* to impart specific physical information.

It is important to remember, when using a *ouija board* for communication, that the *control spirit* is also using this *mediumistic* tool for its own learning and growth. It is exciting to communicate with a *spirit* directly, but, in order to gain a full experience of the communication, the learning experience should be a mutual one. Then the *control spirit* will gain information that you, as a physical person, might have to offer.

Control spirits have a different perspective than you do, because they are not in physical bodies. Since they are separate from you nonphysically, they can readily impart insight and information to add to your learning of yourself. They are not all-knowing. In fact, your physical learning is not something they have experienced. You, being the best judge for yourself, should always trust your own *gut response* to any information given by any *spirit* through a *ouija board*. Like your body and your *spirit*, you are two beings, each with a different perspective and each having insight to offer.

When you communicate with a *control spirit* through your own *ouija board* or the *planchette* of another *medium*, be considerate and caring. As with any friends, the learning and sharing of ideas can best be expressed when all involved are loving and kind.

HOW A OUIJA BOARD WORKS

When working a *ouija board* you are using your *mediumistic* ability. One person is the *medium* through which the communication is possible. The *medium* allows his own energy, through his fingertips as he touches the *planchette*, to serve as a connector to the energy of the *control spirit* in the *planchette*. The *planchette* then moves, by this combination of energy, from letter to letter upon the *alphabet board* spelling out words.

Exercise: Using a Ouija Board

To discover who will be the *medium* for the communication, two people should situate themselves comfortably across from each other with the *alphabet board* between them.

If another person is unavailable, situate yourself in a comfortable position and place the *alphabet board* on your lap or on a flat surface before you.

Practice *preliminaries*. Communicate with your body, your *spirit*, and your guides to aid you with the communication. Open your *release channel* and *focal center* and locate your *body center*.

If you do not feel comfortable or ready for the communication, do not attempt to use the *ouija board*.

Place the *planchette* in the center of the *alphabet board*. Communicate with your *guide* to make sure that the *control spirit* is aware of its responsibilities and ready to communicate. If the *control spirit* is having difficulties, wait until your *guide* or *spirit* lets you know the communication is ready to begin.

When all are ready, place the fingertips of one or both hands on either side of the *planchette*. Sense the energy of the *control spirit*. If two people are using the *ouija board*, one person will sense the energy more clearly than the other. This person will be the *medium* for the duration of the communication.

By sensing the *control spirit's* energy, you allow yourself and the *control spirit* to become acquainted. Trust your *gut response* whenever you place your fingertips upon a *planchette* for communication purposes. If the energy does not feel comfortable to you, remove your hand(s) and communicate with your *spirit* or *guides*. *Release* any *excess energy* into an inanimate object and through your *release channel*.

You are under no obligation to communicate with a *spirit* that is unfavorable to you. Ask your *guide* or *spirit* to help you find a new *control spirit* and enlist their assistance in helping the former *control spirit* remove its energy from the *planchette*.

You do not divorce yourself from any *spirit* by simply putting the *ouija board* away. If you do not communicate with your *guide* or *spirit*, the *control spirit* may remain with the *planchette*. By gaining the help of those close to you on a nonphysical level you can then have a clear *planchette* for another *control spirit* to enter.

If for any reason during the communication, you feel uncomfortable with the *control spirit,* communicate with your *spirit* and *guide* to help you understand and ease your discomfort. If the *control spirit* refuses to leave the *planchette,* follow the instructions defined in the previous chapter for *exorcism.*

Once you have a comfortable feeling about the *control spirit* and the *medium* has been decided upon, the communication may begin.

Keeping your fingertips on the *planchette,* resting them lightly on either side, allow the *planchette* to move across the *alphabet board.* As the *planchette* moves toward a letter, the *medium* should look at the letters on the *alphabet board.* The *medium* is a physical contact for the *control spirit* and will be using his own voice, hand(s), and eyes to help with the communication.

Allow the *planchette* to stop before or over a letter. The *medium* should then verbalize the letter. The *planchette* will continue to stop over or before letters on the *alphabet board.* Each letter should be expressed until a word is formed. Each word will be added to communicate a sentence or thought. When the sentence, or word, or thought is complete, the *planchette* will move to a blank space on the *alphabet board* before beginning a new thought.

Since it is the first time the *control spirit* is working with you or possibly working on any *ouija board,* it may not move the *planchette* at all. You may want to have the *control spirit* move the *planchette* around the *alphabet board,* at first, just to gain a mutual sense of each other. If communication still is difficult, ask a simple question of the *control spirit* out loud. The questions are not limited to the *medium.* The other person participating may also ask questions as long as each question is clear and distinct from the other.

The sole purpose for the *medium* is to use his energy to

aid movement of the *planchette* and communicate words and sentences given. With practice, the *medium* will be able to receive letters, words, or sentences inside his head before they are spelled out on the *alphabet board*. The *control spirit*, having a good working relationship with the *medium*, can then verify the correct information by spelling out the word "Yes," or by giving some other indicator of correct information upon the *alphabet board*.

Continue to ask questions until you receive answers, or allow the *control spirit* to spell out messages until the *planchette* stops. Remember to let the *control spirit* ask questions or suggest ways to increase the process of mutual communication. You will find the most suitable way of communicating with the *control spirit*. In time, the mutual communication will be smooth and understandable for both of you.

A *control spirit* can also allow other *spirits* to communicate through its *planchette* when the *medium* is willing. During such times, the *control spirit* leaves the *planchette*, attaching its energy to it, and with the help of *guides*, the other communicating spirit enters the *planchette* and transmits its message.

When the communication is concluded, the other *spirit* leaves and the *control spirit* returns to the *planchette*. This should only be done when the *control spirit* has a good sense of the process. Your *guide* or *spirit* can be helpful in instructing the *control spirit*. By allowing other *spirits* to use the *planchette*, you will be able to communicate with loved ones, *guides*, and other nonphysical beings more fully for a limited amount of time.

When all communication is completed the *control spirit* may remain or leave the *planchette*, much the way your *spirit* leaves your body when you sleep, always retaining a part of its energy.

After communication, the *medium* and partner should

release excess energy into an inanimate object and through *release channels* before putting away the *ouija board.*

During communications, it is helpful to keep in a journal a dated record of all information given. If a question arises about the information or a prediction comes true, you will have a handy reference to consult.

A *control spirit* is not an authority on any information given. As with any *reading,* you, the recipient, are the best judge for you. It is your responsibility to accept or reject any information or insight offered. By relinquishing this responsibility you lessen your options and ways of learning. Communication is a sharing by those involved. Do not compensate for erroneous predictions or information. Use what is helpful and continue to share information to gain more clarity and perspective.

Before attempting to use a *ouija board* yourself, it would be of benefit for you to watch an experienced *medium* use this tool. Although *ouija boards* are readily available to the public, not everyone uses them correctly. If you have any doubts about using a *ouija board* before, during, or after communication, consult a *medium* practiced in using this tool to get the best physical results.

DAILY USES FOR A OUIJA BOARD

If you are just beginning to use your *mediumistic* ability, a *ouija board* is a good learning tool. It will enable you to gain a stronger sense of your own *mediumistic* process and the presence of your *spirit* and *guides. Ouija boards* can be used to gather knowledge about your past, present, or future as well as to communicate with *spirits* other than yourself. Your *control spirit* can give you a new perspective about nonphysical energy as well as aid you with insights when discovering your own physical blocks to your learnings. By meeting and communicating with this new nonphysical friend, you can add more insight to your daily activities.

Using a *ouija board* can be an enlivening and exciting experience. When used properly it can be instructive and helpful to you throughout your entire life.

Questions and Answers

What if the control spirit *wants to leave the* planchette *and go on to other learnings?*

This is a possibility with which you have no right to interfere. As a friend, you can lovingly help the *control spirit* to continue with its own way of growing. Before the *control spirit* leaves the *planchette,* it should work with your *spirit* and *guides* to find a suitable replacement. When the new *control spirit* is working with you through the *planchette,* the initial *control spirit* can, from time to time, communicate through it with you, if mutually desired.

Why would we use a ouija board *for communication rather than use* semi-trance *or* full-trance communication *ourselves?*

Communication with a *ouija board* exists outside the body and is thus easier to handle and work with when first exploring *mediumistic* ability. *Semi-trance* and *full-trance communication* involve specific time and preparation to experience each fully. *Ouija board communication,* like *indirect voice communication,* can be more flexible and readily available to you.

Can ghosts *use* ouija boards?

Since *ghosts* are not conscious energy forms, they cannot communicate. The energy left behind by a *spirit* may be physical enough to move an object like a *planchette,* but the *planchette's* movement will be without direction and will not be able to spell out a message.

Can two spirits *communicate with each other through separate* ouija boards?

If two *spirits*, with the consent of the *control spirits* involved, wish to communicate through *ouija boards*, they can do so. One *spirit*, using the *planchette*, can communicate through a *medium*. The other *spirit*, using the other *planchette* and *medium*, can then respond. If two *spirits* wish to communicate with each other using only one *planchette*, the first *spirit*, with the help of the *control spirit*, can use the *planchette* and then leave the *planchette*. The second *spirit* can then enter the *planchette* and respond. Communication of both types can continue depending on the willingness of the *spirits*, the *control spirit(s)*, and the *medium(s)*. When all communication is concluded, the *control spirit* returns to the *planchette*.

How long can a control spirit *use a* ouija board *for communication?*

Any mutual learning depends on the people, both physical and nonphysical, involved. There is no time limit for use of a *ouija board* by a *control spirit*. If you, as the *medium*, decide to no longer use the *ouija board* as a learning tool, the *control spirit* can remain with the *planchette* and allow another *medium* to work with it. If the *control spirit* decides to leave a *planchette*, it should then find a replacement if the *medium* wishes to continue to use it for communication.

twelve

OTHER TOOLS OF THE PSYCHIC

Along with the *ouija board* and *crystal ball*, there are many tools that can be used to aid you when practicing your psychic abilities. These tools are not replacements for your own abilities, but they can, in very physical ways, enhance and focus the information received.

It is a misconception to believe that you cannot develop or use your psychic abilities without psychic tools, or that without these tools your psychic abilities will be lessened. Sometimes, by relying on the tools rather than your own natural abilities, you inhibit the amount of information you are capable of generating. You become lazy and resist relying on your inventiveness and experimentation with your natural abilities.

The tools are to be used as stepping stones to reach more of your psychic ability inside yourself. Like a hammer is to a carpenter or a hoe to a gardener, these tools can help you build and cultivate the growth of your own psychic potential. Without your abilities, the tools are meaningless and limited. You house within you the best tool, yourself. The more you work with yourself in developing your psychic abilities the more each tool can aid you.

When you use a psychic tool, it does not give you added importance or detract from your potential. If you are a *medium* who uses a *ouija board* for communication rather than *semi-trance* or *full-trance communication*, you are still a *medium*. The *ouija board* is the tool you feel most comfortable using. It is not a measure of your psychic ability.

Some people will feel comfortable using a specific psychic tool. Others will feel comfortable using several tools. Many will develop and use their psychic abilities alone without ever using any tools. Whatever tool you feel most comfortable using is the best tool for you. Your main objective is to avoid becoming so involved with the process of using the tool that you forget why you are using it.

By trying various tools you will find which will benefit you. If you are attracted to several tools, learn how to use each and try incorporating their use into your *readings*. The boundaries you create for yourself, with or without psychic tools, are those blocks that will inhibit your natural abilities. Psychic tools, when used conscientiously, can help you to develop and further your psychic abilities.

PSYCHIC TOOLS

The best measure to follow when choosing a tool to advance your psychic abilities is your own interest. If you are curious about a specific psychic tool, you should learn about it and explore the possibilities of using it along with your psychic abilities. Listed below are specific tools used professionally by *psychic readers* and *mediums*. Explore those in which you are interested and try to devise your own personal use of them when giving *readings*.

DEVELOP YOUR PSYCHIC ABILITIES

Horoscope

An *astrological* birth chart depicts the exact date, place, and time of birth of a person. Using *astrology,* the science of determining character and potential by mathematically calculating the position of the planets at the time of birth, you can create a *horoscope* to examine the person's talents, problems, personality, future possibilities, and other aspects of his life. Adding your *psychic, mediumistic* or *clairvoyant* abilities to the reading of the *horoscope* can help to focus your psychic abilities. Classes given by professional *astrologers* and books written about the subject can aid you in learning how to chart and use a *horoscope.*

Dream Interpretation

Finding trends and symbols common to your dreams, you can read and understand your own psychic interpretations of your dreams or the dreams of others and how they apply to life. By studying and writing down dream memories, one can gain insight into levels of direction, communications, fears, strengths, abilities, and future possibilities. *Dream interpretations* use many psychic talents including *clairvoyance, mediumship,* and *psychic reading.*

Kirlian Photography

By capturing the *aura* on light-sensitized film you can explore your creative abilities as well as interpret aspects of a person's health, personality, problems, and future projections using your *aura reading* ability, *mediumistic* and *clairvoyant* talents.

Other Tools of the Psychic

Tarot Cards

Seventy-eight symbolic playing-size cards are placed in formations to depict past, present, and future considerations. Depending on the cards chosen, layout of cards, placement of card, and its symbolic meaning, you can relate aspects of a person and his life to him using your *psychic*, *psychometric*, and *clairvoyant* abilities. Chinese, Egyptian, and Indian *tarot cards* are only a few of the types of cards used. Regular playing cards can be used also to relate information significant to the person or situation.

I Ching

The *Chinese Book of Change* is an ancient method for divining insight into the future, or gaining information about a present or past situation. A hexagram is constructed by the toss of three coins in six successions or by throwing the yarrow sticks. The resulting information corresponding to the hexagram in the *I Ching* can be examined by using your *psychic*, *psychometry*, and *aura reading* ability.

Numerology

The *numerologist*, or number reader, can relate the numbers 0–9 to the corresponding letters of a name and number of a birth date or important date in the person's life to gain insight and information about the person. The *numerologist*, through mathematical calculation and use of *psychic*, *psychometric*, and *clairvoyant* abilities, can give *readings* on the person's talents, problems, and potentials plus past, present, and future information.

Handwriting Analysis

A *psychometrist* can look at or hold the handwriting of a person and give valuable information based on the placement of the letters and the way they are written. Strengths, weaknesses, talents, relationships, and future potential can be related using *aura* and *psychic reading* abilities along with *psychometric* talents.

Palmistry

The overall study of the hand(s), used to give information about a person's past, present, future, and nonphysical potential. By tracing and reading various lines and areas of one or both palms and fingers, a *palmist* can gain insights about the person through *psychic, psychometric, clairvoyant,* and *mediumistic* abilities.

Biorhythms

The means of charting daily schedules on a mental, physical, and emotional level for a person by using his birth date and other pertinent information about him. By compiling daily cycles in these three areas, the *reader* can predict patterns and times when the person may be prone to suffer problems or be advised to start new directions. Using *psychic* and *psychometric* abilities, a *biorhythm reader* can give insight and focus to help a person become more aware of current daily patterns and future possibilities.

Automatic Writing

A *mediumistic* tool that involves the use of paper and pencil or typewriter to document communication relayed by *direct voice* or *semi-trance communication.* This written communication from *spirits* can help give impressions to predict possibilities, clarify past information, and gain awareness of present situations.

Pendulum

A small stone or crystal attached to a string is held, by the hand of a *medium,* over a series of letters, objects, pictures, or a person to give information about the person. The *pendulum,* similar to a *ouija board planchette,* moves in designated patterns over the object(s) to communicate nonphysical insights about the past, present, or future. The *medium* reads these circular, horizontal, or vertical movements in response to a question asked, adding other insights or information coming from the *communicating spirit.*

Psychic Drawing

The construction of a picture, rendered by an artist, representing both nonphysical and physical aspects of a person. By using *aura reading* and *mediumistic* and *clairvoyant* abilities, the artist interprets the energy of the person in shapes, colors, and symbols.

Tea Leaves

A combination of loose tea leaves and hot water is stirred according to direction and then ingested by the person being read. When all of the liquid is absorbed, the cup is inverted on the saucer and the excess tea leaves are removed. Those tea leaves adhering to the cup are then read according to their configurations and positions on the inside of the cup. By using *psychic, clairvoyant, psychometric* and *mediumis-*

tic abilities, the *reader* gives information about the person's past, present, or future, or any question asked.

Past Life Reading

Using *clairvoyant* and *mediumistic* abilities, a *past-life reader* can give information related to present situations and future possibilities by exploring past experiences and talents.

There are many more tools of the *psychic* and combinations of tools that can be used for focus with your own psychic abilities. Before using any tool, study it and understand the best way you can incorporate it into the use of your own abilities. Investigate techniques and tools used by other *readers* to gain a better perspective about these tools. After you have explored, researched, and observed the use of these tools, allow your own natural tendencies to incorporate them into your *readings*. They will not replace your own natural talents. They will only expand them.

Questions and Answers

What if I cannot find a tool I wish to try to use? What if no tool is available to me?

Devise your own version of the tool, constructing and using it according to your needs. Experiment with your own creativity. The tool, itself, was devised by someone initially in the same situation. By using your natural talents you may refine an already existing tool or create a new one which will work well for you.

Will I confuse myself if I use or try many tools?

Feel free to observe and try the tools that attract you. In time and with practice, some tools will become more comfortable to use than others. Let your *gut response* help you as you experiment with each tool that interests you. Work with one tool at a time until you wish to eliminate it or until you feel comfortable and competent to use it within your *readings*.

How will I know if I am becoming too dependent on a tool?

When you find yourself unable to read or give viable impressions without the tool, you are depending upon it for your own credibility. When you find yourself making excuses for your psychic abilities based on your use of the tool(s), you are not relying on yourself. When you are able to use the same ability with or without the tool, and find the tool to be an added aid for focus, you are using the tool(s) productively.

How can I avoid readers who use tools as gimmicks to prove their psychic abilities?

By experiencing and studying the proper use of psychic tools yourself, you will be able to know when a person is misusing the tool(s) or relying on them in a fraudulent manner. Your *gut response* will help you quickly if, in fact, the use of the tool(s) or the information is not valid for you.

thirteen

WHAT TO LOOK FOR IN A COMPETENT READER

Many people visit a professional *psychic reader*, *medium*, *healer*, *numerologist*, *psychometrist*, *tea-leaf reader*, and others to learn more about themselves, the people close to them, and their potential. The *psychic* field is filled with honest and talented professional people whose aim is to provide accurate and useful information to help people with their daily lives.

It is also a field rife with frauds posing as *readers*, or *readers* who use their psychic abilities to manipulate and deceive the public. As in psychology, sociology, medicine or any humanistic-oriented field, the added problems of personal shortcomings, egos, and dogma prevail. Since the *psychic* profession is involved often with much that is physically intangible, people are intrigued and sometimes led astray by misinformation. The question to be asked is not whether you should consider seeing a *reader* for gaining insight about yourself but how to choose a *competent reader*.

HOW TO CHOOSE A COMPETENT READER

You decide to see a professional *reader* in order to gain insight about a problem you are having, to discover more about your talents and potential, or to experience a professional *reading*. How can you accomplish this?

Like most professionals, *competent readers* in the psychic field do not advertise. Since *readings* are private and personal, there is no objective measure of the quality of *readers* available to the general public. One way to compensate for this is to ask people who have gone to *readers* to recommend one to you. Keep in mind that this is a subjective process. What may be good for one person may not necessarily be good for another. Try asking several people about a *reader* in question, or find books or articles written by or about that *reader*. If the *reader* is teaching a class or giving a lecture nearby, try to attend to gain your own sense of the person. By trusting your *gut response* upon meeting the *reader*, you will sense if a *reading* given by this person will be of benefit to you. If you are able to find something written by the *reader*, hold his or her book or article, photograph or brochure, and, using your own psychic abilities, read the person to determine if he or she would be a good *reader* for you.

If you have no alternative but the suggestion of a friend or acquaintance, call the *reader* on the telephone to find out specific information about the *reading* itself: What abilities he will be using, duration of the *reading*, his related experience in the field, number of years he has been reading, and price of the *reading*.

By conversing with the *reader* you will gain a sense of and have a *gut response* to him. If you get a positive *gut response* to the person and feel interested in having a *reading*, then the *reading* probably will be a worthwhile experience for you. If you feel hesitant, even when several people have spoken favorably about the *reader*, trust your own responses for they will prove to be most meaningful for you. Wait to schedule an appointment for a *reading* so that you can give yourself time to discover your own personal reactions to having the *reading* itself, and your feelings about the *reader* and his or her competency.

Once you have found the desired *reader* and have scheduled an appointment, what can you expect from the *reader* during the *reading?*

WHAT TO LOOK FOR
IN A COMPETENT READER

Many of the suggestions offered in "Do's and Don'ts When Reading" (Chapter 3) apply when being given a professional *reading*. It is now your turn to sit back and experience your own *reading* from a total stranger.

1. A *competent reader* needs no specific atmosphere or props or gimmickry such as: costumes, objects, candles, or dark rooms in order to work effectively. The aura of mystery may be stimulating but is not needed. A valid *reader* should be able to give impressions in any surrounding. It is more conducive to work in a quiet atmosphere without distraction, but external crutches separate from the *reader's* own tools: *tarot cards, tea leaves, astrological charts, crystal balls,* or *ouija boards*, should not be factors in delivering accurate and honest information. He or she should be able to use the abilities described to you before the *reading* anytime and anywhere the *reading* occurs.

2. A *competent reader* should be consistent when giving information. There is no such thing as an "off" day for a *reader* unless he or she is physically ill or emotionally or

mentally upset. In that event, the *reader* should ask to re-schedule the reading.

3. A *competent reader* should be able to read for any-one, regardless of personal beliefs. As long as the person being read is not closed or hostile to the *reader,* the *reading* should be given. If a *reader* is unwilling to read for anyone without a realistic excuse or refuses to read for people whose personal beliefs do not coincide with his own, that *reader's* abilities should be questioned.

4. A *competent reader* should be open and honest about the way in which the *reading* is done. He or she should be willing to answer questions about information given and about the use of his or her abilities related to the *reading.* The *reader* should be willing to explain the type of *reading* used or add insight when possible to information received, if requested to do so. If such information is not forthcoming, this should be clearly stated.

5. A good *reader* will not edit or expand information. A *competent reader* should allow all insights received to stand on their own merits, and should readily admit when he or she is not receiving any information about a given subject. There should be no creation of false impressions to mislead or please you during a *reading.* Vague state-ments that could mislead or confuse you should not be added to replace lack of information received or to fulfill the scheduled time period for the *reading.* The *reader* should not alter or delete any information coming through during the *reading* for you. It is the *reader's* responsibility to be honest during the entire *reading.*.

6. A valid *reader* needs no previous knowledge or in-formation about you before or during a *reading.* If in the process of the *reading,* additional information is requested of you for clarification of insights given or to gain a clear focus about a situation, it is your option to provide it. Be wary of a *reader* who uses the information you have added to manipulate you at a later time in the *reading*.

You should not feel pressed to give the *reader* any additional information. If you decide to furnish the *reader* with additional information during your *reading*, and the *reader* adds no insight or does not use this information as a stepping stone to continue with other impressions coming to him, the validity of that *reader* should be questioned.

7. A *reader* should never use information or impressions received to manipulate you or to gain added power or money. For example, if a *reader* gives valid information about you and then manipulates further information to reinforce the belief that a curse has been put on you or a member of your family, or that negative energy is around you and then suggests that, for a substantial fee, he or she can eliminate the disturbance for you, be wary. This type of situation is not uncommon. The *reader's* primary impressions are quite valid. What the *reader* does with the information is dishonest.

Most rational people believe that they will not be taken in by such a situation. When you are receiving valid information about yourself from a person who does not know you, how do you then decide that the information that follows is not valid? The answer is to trust your own *gut response* to all information you are receiving from a *reader*.

Do not assume that every *reader* will manipulate information they receive, but if you do encounter such a *reader*, your *gut response* will permit you to benefit from valid information and discard what does not apply to you.

8. A *reader* should not impose his or her own personal beliefs, techniques, or philosophy upon you during the *reading*. If the *reader* is religiously, morally, or philosophically for or against any information given, he or she should be able to keep personal feelings or prejudices out of the way of the information being received.

This does not mean that you cannot benefit from a *reading* given by a person whose beliefs or orientation differs from your own. A *competent reader* will not allow such feelings to interfere with the information given to you during your *reading*. When this does occur, your own *gut response* will automatically help you sort through subjective interpretations.

9. It is the responsibility of the *reader* to allow you the full time designated for the *reading* without physical interferences. Phone calls, visits from family or friends, or other intrusions during the course of the *reading* should not occur. You also have the option of having someone present with you during your *reading* as long as they are courteous and do not interfere with the *reading*. Bear in mind that the *reading* might involve very personal information about you and that you might want the privacy of discussing these impressions alone with the reader.

10. A *competent reader* should always allow you to tape or record the *reading* in some manner. If, in the course of *full-trance communication*, the noise from the tape recorder distracts the *medium*, you should be allowed to take written notes. Any *reader* who does not allow the *reading* to be documented by the person who is receiving it, should be questioned and a plausible excuse must be given for this denial.

A professional *reader*, regardless of the psychic abilities used during a *reading*, should conduct himself or herself similarly to any other professional rendering a service. *Readers* are not authority figures. They share their talents, like many other people, to provide help and insight to you. They should be treated with human respect and consideration. The *reader's* sole purpose is to transfer information and impressions in an open, clear, and honest manner to you. Your responsibility is to be willing to listen to, and accept or reject any information offered. When a *reading* is conducted in this manner, you will not be misguided, deceived, or ignorant about information being given by a *reader*.

When you are being read by a professional *reader*, remember that it is your *reading*. If you feel strongly against the way in which the *reading* is conducted, or reactive to the information being given, check your *gut response* to see if you are being defensive about information that applies to your growing. If you are not being defensive about the information, but feel manipulated by the *reader*, voice your complaint(s) to the *reader* to help rectify the situation. If the situation persists, it is your option to conclude the *reading* or allow it to continue, taking from it the information that is valid for you.

The days of dark rooms, fear, frauds, and worship of powerful figures is fast diminishing. The possibilities of sharing of impressions and insights in a positive and honest atmosphere far outweigh trepidations and can benefit all involved.

Questions and Answers

What do I do when I get two different messages from two different readers?

If you listen to the tapes of your *readings* or compare notes taken, you may find that the essence of the information is the same for both *readings,* and only the way in which the information is expressed is different. If the messages do not agree at all and are diametrically opposed, rely on your *gut response* when rereading or hearing each *reading* to determine what information applies best and is most helpful to you.

If I go to a psychic fair *where there are many* readers *available, how will I know which* reader *to choose?*

Psychic fairs usually are held in a large room or area of a shopping mall or arena, where all of the *readers* are identified and seated near each other. Walk around the area where the *readers* are and watch them as they give their *readings.* Trusting your *gut response,* you will be drawn to or interested in one or more *readers.* If you find yourself interested in several *readers* and only wish to have one *reading,* hold a card or available brochure of each *reader* separately and use your own psychometric ability to help you decide which one to choose. The more you trust your *gut response* and your own natural psychic abilities and are not influenced by the *reader's* press notices, tools, or physical characteristics, the better chance you will have of finding a good *reader* for you.

Is there a time period to wait between readings?

Since a *reading* is about you, the information generated may need some time to be sorted through and rejected or applied. If you wish to have the added benefit of additional insight from another *reader* or want to return to the same *reader* shortly after the first *reading,* that is entirely up to you. There is no designated time limit between *readings.*

Is it better to be read by a specific type of reader?

The type of *reading* you have is your own personal preference. Some people prefer being read by *astrologers* or *tarot card readers* rather than *aura readers* or *mediums.* If you feel drawn to a *reader* who uses a certain tool, then follow your *gut response.* If a person calls himself an *astrologer,* he should use your *horoscope* and/or other *astro-*

logical tools within the *reading*. Many *readers* are multi-talented and do not limit themselves to only one psychic ability when giving a *reading*. Do not limit yourself by exteriors. Any variation of a tool or ability can be used within a *reading* as long as the *reader* uses the abilities in which he claims to be skilled.

What is the average price for a reading?

As with any profession, the relative price for a *reading* depends on the service rendered, the time spent, the *reader's* experience and skill, and the personal choice of the *reader*. Readings can range from two dollars to more than $500. The amount of money for the *reading* should be decided upon before the *reading* is given, unless otherwise discussed with the *reader*. The amount of money designated may not be commensurate with the priceless, and sometimes immeasurable, help offered.

fourteen

PSYCHOKINESIS

Superman, a comic book hero, was able to move mountains, stop speeding bullets, and leap tall buildings in a single bound. In essence, it was believed he was using his psychokinetic ability. Surely Superman's supposed talent was highly developed, but *psychokinesis* is not a fantasy. It is the ability to affect physical matter, moving or altering its state, without the use of mechanical or physical means.

People often refer to *psychokinesis* as the power of mind over matter. The true source for this ability is not mental, but is nonphysical energy. Just as Superman focused his energy from his *focal center* or *third eye*, you can affect your own environment by using your psychokinetic ability.

The physical results derived from using *psychokinesis* are tangible enough to prompt the Soviet government to invest large sums of money to establish tests and to experiment with the development of this ability. It is believed that tests using *psychokinesis* are being considered for use to aid in defense preparations for the advent of war.

Psychokinesis is thought to have been used to erect large temples of worship and edifices for mankind throughout the development of civilization. Such structures, being studied by scholars all over the world, may have been built by using a process of *psychokinesis* called *levitation:* The ability to raise and move large pieces of physical matter without physical effort.

Some of the most intriguing structures known to the physical world are said to have possibly been erected in this manner. The Great Pyramids, Egyptian crypts, Stonehenge in England, Machu Picchu in Peru, and airstrips on the Nazca Plains are believed to have been built by using *levitation.*

Pyramids are designed structurally according to specific mathematical calculations. By erecting them in this manner, the energy force created inside the pyramid can be made to affect any physical object or person placed inside it. Sarcophaguses remaining within these pyramids for thousands of years have, upon exhumation, revealed little or no alternation to their basic form or content.

Numerous books written about pyramids give explicit directions for the creation of such structures according to scale. If you are able to visit a pyramid or create one of your own, following mathematical specifications, you may wish to experience or test the energy force created inside such a structure. Once the pyramid is erected, place an unsharpened pencil or razor blade in the very center of the pyramid. Leave the pencil or razor untouched in this position for a period of time. Observe the object daily and keep a journal of your observations. In time you will find that the razor edge or pencil point will be sharpened without physical effort.

If the pyramid is large enough for you to sit inside it, practice *preliminaries* and allow yourself to remain in its center to sense or feel the energy flow created. This energy will not hurt you. Any additional energy retained after leaving the pyramid can be expelled through your *release channel* and from your hands into an inanimate object.

When you want to move, bend, straighten, or alter a physical object by using your psychokinetic ability, you are simply adding your nonphysical energy in a directed way to affect the object. The difference between affecting an object using *psychokinesis* and releasing energy into an inanimate object involves focus and direction of the energy flow. When you release energy you are dispersing it. When you use your psychokinetic ability you are directing your energy and giving focus to it.

Exercise: Bending a Physical Object

Place before you a key, spoon, fork, or any small metal object on a flat surface. A metal object is suggested because it is not fragile or pliable and cannot easily be altered physically. Be sure that the utensil, key, or object is not important to you because its shape may be altered during the exercise.

Practice *preliminaries: release excess energy, total relaxation* and *collect* your *energy*. Communicate with your body and *spirit* to help you during the exercise. Open your *release channel* to relieve yourself of excessive energy accumulated. Open your *focal center* and allow your energy to flow through it. When you sense or feel the energy flow through your *focal center,* you are ready to begin.

Look at the object resting before you. Which way do you want to affect it? Do you want to bend it in its center? Do you want to bend down the right side? Do you want it to bend in more than one place? Determine which way you wish to alter the object.

Clear your mind of all thoughts and visualize the object bent according to your direction.

Take the object into your hand or hands or let it rest directly in front of you on the table. Send your energy, through your *focal center,* directly to the area on the object you wish to affect. Keep visualizing the final result or the process of the object bending.

If you want to use your hands and fingers to help you affect the physical object, hold the object in one or both hands and stroke it vigorously at the place where you want to bend it. If this is uncomfortable, run your fingers along the area you want it to bend or hold the object in your open hand(s) allowing the energy from your hands and fingers, as well as your *focal center,* to bend the object. Experiment with several techniques until you find the one most comfortable and effective for you.

If you find yourself losing focus or the visual picture of the bent object, relax, clear your mind, and try again. The more you push to physically affect the object, the less chance it will have to bend. By relaxing, visualizing, and focusing energy, you will alter the energy of the object and it will bend.

Continue this exercise until you sense the energy lessening from your *focal center,* or hands, or you sense that you wish to stop the exercise. Your focus during the exercise should be on affecting the shape of the object. Each time you interrupt your energy flow to study or notice any changes in the object's physical nature you will find that you will have to start the process over again. The focus of energy works best in a cumulative fashion. Any interference disturbs the continuity of the process.

When you have finished, place the object down upon the table and study it. Has it changed in shape or appearance? If so, has it bent in the way you visualized?

Leave the object alone for a short while and return to it later. Upon returning to the object, you may find it has bent further. The energy within the object will continue to affect it after the exercise is completed.

If the object has not changed shape, you may repeat the exercise for additional results.

Exercise: Moving a Physical Object

This exercise can be experienced alone or with a group of people.

Place a piece of blank paper on a table or desk a short distance from those participating in the exercise. If a group of people is used, have each person seat himself comfortably, equidistant from the paper, within a semicircle.

Place a chopstick or pencil horizontally upon the center of the paper. Trace the outline of the pencil or chopstick on the paper to have a linear indicator of its position.

Before beginning the exercise, decide which way you want to move the object: clockwise or counter clockwise, forward or backward, left or right. Decide also on which place on the object you wish to focus. In a group situation, a common consensus can be used. It is important that all members of the group are focusing their energies to affect the movement of the object in the same way. Otherwise conflicting energy directions will impede the movement of the object.

People involved in the exercise should practice *preliminaries* and communicate with their bodies and *spirits* to gain help with their focus. Open *release channels* and *focal centers*, clear your minds and visualize the pencil or chopstick moving in the intended direction.

Allow the energy from the *focal center* to flow toward the object to the place you wish to affect.

If you find yourself pushing or blocking your energy by trying too hard, or becoming distracted during the exercise, relax, clear your mind, and try again to allow the energy to flow freely from your *focal center* to the object.

Keep visualizing the object moving and sending energy from your *focal center* until you wish to stop. If you would like to use your hands during the exercise to help you add to your energy flow, place them in front of you pointed toward the object. Focus all energy at the place on the object you wish to affect.

If you are working in a group, the exercise is concluded when all members have finished transmitting energy or when a designated time period for the exercise has lapsed.

Examine the object and its position on the paper. Has it moved beyond the lines drawn? Has it moved in the intended direction? The object should not be touched after the exercise is completed so that any energy remaining inside it may continue to affect it.

Repeat this exercise as often as desired, being sure to practice *preliminaries* and other processes before beginning again.

The same exercise can be tried with a slight variation.

Place a pencil or a chopstick in a vertical position in a cup or glass. Be sure that at least one-third of the object is visible to all people participating in the exercise. Mark the glass or cup at the point where the object rests against it and gently place the cup on a table in the middle of the semicircle of people. Check to see if the object is resting in its designated place before beginning.

Agree upon whether to move the object in a clockwise or counter clockwise direction. Then practice *preliminaries* and, for best results, repeat the same procedures suggested in the previous exercise.

Exercise: Moving a Large Object in a Group Setting

One person, using his psychokinetic ability, can move a heavy object. This exercise uses the additional energy of others to achieve movement.

A large round table is needed for this exercise.

Situate each person comfortably around the table so that they can touch fingertips. A wooden table or one made from natural materials is preferred so that the energy will be conducted rather than dissipated. A picnic table with slats would be a good choice, the slats being easy markers for noting movement. A paper tablecloth, or pieces of paper with lines drawn to serve as markers, can be attached to the table top if a picnic table is not available.

Before beginning this exercise, a group consensus should decide whether to move the table clockwise or counter clockwise.

All group members should practice *preliminaries,* remembering to *release excess energy* into inanimate objects and not into the table, communicate with body and *spirit,* and open *release channels* and *focal centers.*

When ready, each person then can place both hands flat upon the table with palms down. Fingers should extend so that the little finger of each hand touches the little finger of those seated on either side. Relax hands, so they are resting comfortably upon the surface of the table. With fingers touching, clear your minds.

Visualize the table moving in the direction intended. Allow all energy to flow through both hands and *focal centers* to the table.

If, during this exercise, a person feels blocked or wishes to separate himself from the exercise, he can withdraw his hands slowly and reconnect the fingers of the two people next to him. This ensures the continuity of the flow of energy from the group into the table. If you cannot tell if you are blocking your energy, remain in position and use your *gut response* and body communication to assist you. By communicating with your body, you can rectify your problem and continue with the exercise. If you leave the circle at the table, do not reenter until the experiment is concluded or another has begun, so as not to disturb the energy flow already in progress.

When all members sense a lessening of energy flow or the designated time for the exercise is completed, take your hands from the table and *release excess energy* into an inanimate object.

Check results to see if the slats or lines on the table have moved during the exercise. Do not remove the lines or alter the position of the table for a period of time after the exercise is concluded. Check for additional results before beginning the exercise again.

Exercise: Levitating a Large Object in a Group Setting

To achieve *levitation*, a slightly different process is needed.

One person should be seated in a chair without arms for easy accessibility.

All other people involved in the exercise should place themselves in a close semicircle around the chair, leaving the front of the chair free for the person to sit comfortably.

Each member of the group should practice *preliminaries*, communicate with body and *spirit*, and open *release channel* and *focal center* to allow energy to flow.

The first person standing, beginning on the right side of the chair, should extend his open hand, palm down, and hold it slightly above the center of the seated person's head. The next person should repeat the procedure, placing his hand directly above the first hand, a slight distance apart from it. Each person, in succession, should repeat this exercise forming a line of hands, palms down, directly above the center of the seated person's head.

The first person should, in the same manner, then place his other hand directly above the hand of the last person. Each person should repeat the exercise until both hands of each person are directly above the person's head in order of succession. This vertical line of extended hands will produce a force of energy to affect the levitation of the person seated.

Using *focal centers* and hands, each person in the semicircle should remain in this position for a short time to allow the energy force to flow and build.

When ready, the top hand should be withdrawn slowly from the line of energy and placed near the person's side. Each hand, in turn, should be removed from its previous position until all within the semicircle are resting their hands near their sides.

Each person should then place his index and middle fingers together on both hands. Quickly place these fingers underneath the outer edges of the chair and lift together. If this is done properly, the person seated will be lifted with little or no effort.

When trying this exercise, remember that the result is dependent on the accumulation of the energy force created by the group. Losing focus or blocking energy can disturb the initial attempt at *levitation*. If such a problem occurs for any member of the group during the exercise, begin the exercise again, rather than resume it from the point at which the problem occurs.

If you do not wish to levitate a person in a chair, a small but heavy table will serve as a replacement. Repeat the entire procedure each time you attempt this exercise.

Be sure to *release excess energy* accumulated through your hands into an inanimate object and through *release channels* after the exercise is concluded.

If you do not want to practice *psychokinesis* in a group situation and would like to use this talent practically, there are several exercises to follow.

Exercise: Adjusting Your Television Set Using Psychokinesis

When the horizontal or vertical picture on your television set starts to waver and cannot be remedied by adjusting the dial, your psychokinetic ability can help you.

For the purpose of this exercise, set your television dial so that the vertical or horizontal hold on your picture fluctuates. When the picture is steadily fluctuating, place yourself a short distance away from the television. Situate yourself in a comfortable position.

Practice all *preliminaries* and communicate with your body and *spirit* for focus. Open *release channel* and *release excess energy* through your hands into an inanimate object if necessary. Open your *focal center* and allow your energy to flow from the *focal center* to the picture on the television set.

With your mind cleared, visualize the picture moving to an upright steady position. Send energy from your *focal center* to affect the movement of the picture. If you use your hands, as well, place them directly in front of you in a comfortable position, facing the picture on the television screen. Allow all energy to flow through your fingertips to the picture to steady its movements.

If you begin to lose focus, or feel blocked, or find the picture holding and then fluctuating again, relax, clear your mind, and begin again.

Practice this exercise as often as desired or until the picture on the television screen is steady and holding.

Release all *excess energy* from you when the exercise is concluded.

Exercise: Moving a Phonograph Needle
Using Psychokinesis

You may find your phonograph needle stuck in a record groove and want to move it, or, for the purpose of this exercise, you may want to cause the needle to repeat.

When the needle is steadily stuck in the record groove, leave the room and situate yourself in a room nearby.

Practice all *preliminaries*, body and *spirit* communication, and opening of *release channel* and *focal center* before beginning the exercise.

Clear your mind and visualize where you want to move the needle, forward or backward on the record.

Allow your energy to flow from your *focal center* and your hands, if desired, in the direction of the phonograph needle.

Do not push to move the needle, but allow the energy to flow freely from your *focal center* and your hands.

If you feel blocked or distracted during the exercise, relax, visualize the needle again, and allow your energy to flow toward it.

Repeat this exercise as often as desired. *Release* all *excess energy* through your *release channel* and your hands when the exercise is completed.

The more you practice your psychokinetic ability, the more sense you will have of your energy flow and how to use it to affect physical matter.

DAILY USES FOR PSYCHOKINESIS

You may not want to move mountains or stop locomotives, but you can use *psychokinesis* to straighten bent machinery parts or utensils, restart engines or repair broken watches and clocks. Use *psychokinesis* to lessen the physical effort of moving furniture or lifting heavy boxes or grocery bags. *Psychokinesis* can help you pedal your bicycle easily up a steep hill or protect you from a falling tree branch during a storm. Construction materials can be moved and lifted with little effort when you use *levitation* along with your physical strength.

Psychokinesis can be of added benefit when you are busy and need to lower the flame on your stove or want to move the phonograph needle from its stuck position on your favorite record. Sit in your chair and use your psychokinetic ability to dim the hall lights or adjust the picture on your television set. With practice you can even use *psychokinesis* to stop the villains from attacking the hero on your video game. Psychokinesis, used practically, can lessen the physical strain of everyday living and help you to live a comfortable, productive life.

Questions and Answers

Can psychokinesis *be misused, especially during times of war?*

Even when a person or nation is devoted truly to destruction, *psychokinesis* cannot be totally used for war purposes. Since the energy used for *psychokinesis* is shared by everyone, it is naturally balanced and works well in its balanced form. If used in a focused manner for destruction, the natural balance of the energy itself would become imbalanced and less functional. When used productively, *psychokinesis* can be effective in aiding our planet's growth and productivity. Stretching the imagination to the event of nuclear war, a group or nation of people collectively can use *psychokinesis* to stop and return any missile, submarine, or nuclear warhead from its appointed mission. The positive use of this focused energy can block and alter any implement of destruction devised mechanically.

Can our guides *help us with* psychokinesis?

When using any psychic ability, your *guides,* body, and *spirit* can help you focus your energies and use them productively. If you are blocking your energies, your *guide* can give you objective insight to help you to allow your energy to flow more readily. Your *guide* can use its own energy to help you move or lift a physical object. Since your *guide* does not have a physical body to serve as a connector to this level, its energy may not affect physical matter as easily as your own.

Why is there such little use of psychokinesis *to construct buildings as there was during ancient times?*

There are probably many theories concerning this question, but one possibility may be that the sophisticated use of modern technology has focused us away from ourselves and on those things external to us. We have readily developed our intellectual capabilities more than our predecessors and have come to practically rely on them for all aspects of living.

Can psychokinesis *be done while in a* trance *state?*

Just as you use your own energy to move or alter physical matter, the *spirit,* using the body of a *medium,* can use its energy to affect an object. Whether in a *trance* state or inside your own body, the use of this nonphysical energy and its ability to move objects is relative to the *spirit* or person involved.

What do I do when I feel overpowered by the energy I am using to move or lift an object?

If, at any time, you feel overpowered by the force of the energy you are using, focus away from the exercise and *release* all excess energy through your *focal center* and hands. This situation is not hazardous. What has happened is that you have disturbed the balance of energy inside your body by accumulating too much energy during the exercise. By working with your body and *releasing excess energy* when you feel overwhelmed, you can facilitate the body's own natural energy balancing process.

If the object itself is overpowering because your mental image or experience of its weight or size is hampering you, work with your body and focus on the energy, rather than the object, to allow you to lift or move it without effort.

fifteen

TELEPATHY

Phrases like: "You took the words right out of my mouth" or "That's exactly what I was just thinking" apply to *telepathy*. It is the most physically oriented of our psychic abilities. When using *telepathy* one person reads the exact thought, word, or impression from the mind of another. Telepathy is the psychic communication between bodies using their intellectual tool, the mind. A *telepathist*, one who uses *telepathy*, is a mental radar detector, picking up thoughts and allowing them directly inside his mind.

A *telepathic reading* often is confused with a *psychic reading*. When reading a person telepathically you are focused on the exact thought and moment when it arises in the person's mind. This is known only in the immediate present. *Psychic reading* involves impressions about the person's present, past, or future. The information received is not confined to the person's thoughts and can relate to other people in the person's life.

The transference of nonphysical energy changed into

mental body thought happens when two or more people are attuned to this physical process. The person transmitting the word or thought through his mind is called the *sender*. The person receiving the word or thought is called the *receiver*.

Communicating telepathically is like having a voiceless and cordless telephone conversation. The *sender* transmits his thought and the *receiver* accepts it. When both people are open to this form of communication, the number of thoughts transferred is endless.

Some people will have more telepathic ability as *senders;* others will be better *receivers*. Some people will be able to send and receive messages with equal ease. One is not better than the other; each type of ability, like all psychic abilities, is relevant to the person's needs and development.

A *telepathist* does not have any power or control over another person's mental process. He is simply a conduit of nonphysical energy given from the body. The process of *telepathy* includes a willingness of both *sender* and *receiver* to share their mutual body communication. If a friend is suffering from a stressful relationship, you cannot, as a *sender,* place thoughts inside his mind or even stop him from pursuing the relationship. Even if your friend is willing to receive your thoughts, the responsibility to use and act upon them rests with him. Like any psychic ability, *telepathy* is used naturally to help you develop your capabilities. You will find that, when you receive thoughts from another person, you will be able to determine quickly their derivation by trusting your own *gut response* to them. No one can influence you without your own desire to be influenced.

If, while using *telepathy,* you find yourself receiving more than one thought too rapidly, clear your mind, relax, and allow the thought to enter your mind again. If you become too confused during this process, communicate with your body to enlist its help in deciphering messages clearly. Using body communication, you will be able to discover your own mental defenses that prevent you from communicating telepathically.

There are several exercises you can use to discover whether you are a *sender* or a *receiver* without involving you with the personal thoughts of another person.

Exercise: Reading Symbols Telepathically

To use this exercise productively two or more people should participate.

Take several heavy opaque sheets of paper or cardboard and cut them into twenty-five card-size pieces. On each set of five cards, draw a basic symbol such as a circle, square or alphabetical letter. Each set of symbols should be different and legible in size for the group to see. For example: five squares, five circles, five number eights, five stars, five houses.

Select one person to be the *sender* for the exercise. All others should sit comfortably in front of the *sender*, a short distance away so as not to see the cards as they are being read.

All *receivers* should have a pencil and paper before them. Number the paper from 1–25. Reading twenty-five cards is called a *run*. The members of the group should list the five symbols at the top of the paper for reference during the exercise.

The *sender* should *release excess energy* into an inanimate object and then shuffle the cards until all symbols are mixed together. The cards should then be placed face down near the *sender*.

All participants should practice *preliminaries*, open *release channels*, and communicate with their bodies for help in focus. *Focal centers* should be opened to facilitate receiving energy.

Both *sender* and *receivers* should clear their minds of all thoughts before beginning and after each card has been read.

When ready, the *sender* should take the top card and face it toward himself. Focusing on the symbol seen, the *sender* should then send the image of the symbol, word describing it, or a visual picture of it from his mind to the minds of the *receivers*. His energy from the *focal center* will help this process.

The *receivers* should allow themselves, using their *focal centers*, to receive the impression, word, or visual image inside their minds. When an impression is received, the symbol should be written down beside its corresponding number during the run.

After a few minutes have passed, both *sender* and *receivers* should clear their minds and the second card symbol should then be transmitted in the same way.

If you are confused at any time during the exercise or find yourself receiving no impressions, clear your mind and communicate with your body to resolve the problem. If you find yourself receiving more than one impression, word or picture, use your *gut response* for each to help clarify your perceptions.

Continue *sending* and *receiving* until all twenty-five cards are used.

When the *run* is completed, the *sender* should then hold up each card in order before the group for confirmation of results.

When using a deck of twenty-five cards or one *run*, one symbol in five accurately received is accredited to chance or is considered an average score. In one *run*, five cards, accurately received, is average. More than five impressions accurately received is above average. When using 100 cards or four *runs* of the deck of cards, twenty-five accurately received symbols are accredited to chance or are an average score.

Repeat this exercise as often as desired, keeping track of the number of *runs* and allowing time between each card reading.

Some people will score very high during this exercise, others will not. This exercise is not a test of your telepathic ability. It is a way to assist you in developing your ability and achieve accurate results. The problem when using an exercise of this type is that the repetition involved can cause boredom and distraction. By refocusing and relaxing, using the body to help you remain alert, this problem can be diminished greatly.

Exercise: Telepathy Between Two People Using Numbers

Following the same objectives described in the previous exercise, choose one person to be the *sender* and the other to be the *receiver*.

Practice *preliminaries*, open *release channels* and *focal centers*, and communicate with your bodies for aid in focus.

Both people should clear their minds of all thoughts before beginning.

The *sender* should choose a number from 1–30 and focus on that number, sending an impression, word, or visual picture of the number to the *receiver* using the *focal center*.

When the *receiver* has accepted the number compare results.

Repeat this exercise as desired, allowing each partner to be the *sender* and then the *receiver* of numbers.

To accelerate the exercise, expand the range of numbers to include 1–100. If either partner wishes to chart the results in number of *runs*, paper and pencil should be available.

Exercise: Telepathy Between Two People with Objects or Words

A variation of the last exercise involves words or objects chosen by the *sender* to transmit to the *receiver*. This gives each person a wider range of variables from which to choose.

Any word or picture of an object can be used and sent telepathically between the *sender* and *receiver*.

After practicing *preliminaries*, opening body centers, and communicating as before, the *sender* should picture an object or word inside his mind and, using his *focal center*, transmit it to the *receiver*.

When the image is received, the *receiver* should verbalize his impression. Switch positions so both people can experience being *sender* and *receiver*.

Minds of both participants should be cleared before each image, word or visual picture is transmitted to ensure clear focus and communication.

If you wish to record results, a pencil and piece of paper should be available.

Since *telepathy* is a psychic talent, using nonphysical energy, communication can occur between two people regardless of the physical distance between them. To communicate telepathically, you do not even need to know or be intimate with the other person. All you need is a willingness to send or receive information.

Exercise: Long Distance Telepathy

The people involved should agree upon the exact time and date for the communication before beginning the exercise.

One person should be chosen as the *sender*, the other as the *receiver*. If the exercise is repeated at another time, reverse positions during the communication so that each person can experience being both *sender* and *receiver*.

Shortly before the designated time for the communication, each person should practice *preliminaries*, communicate with his body, open *release channel* and *focal center*, and clear his mind of any thoughts.

At the appropriate time, the *sender* can send the chosen message, focusing on a clear mental picture of the image, word or thought(s) that represents it while using his *focal center* to transmit energy to the *receiver*.

The *receiver*, using his *focal center*, then can receive the image, word or thought(s). Relaxing and focusing will produce better results than concentrating and tensing during communication.

Allow several minutes for the transference to take place. After the designated time has passed, contact the other participant to check results.

If you would like to vary this exercise, repeat the same procedure without specifying an exact time or date for the communication. Allow a time frame of a week or a few days to pass, during which the *sender* decides exactly when to send the message without the *receiver's* foreknowledge. This allows for more of the freedom and spontaneity often encountered when using your telepathic ability in daily life. The more practiced you become with this talent, the more frequently it can be used to help you in a natural way.

DAILY USES FOR TELEPATHY

If you are going to be late for dinner or a meeting and have no access to a telephone, send your message telepathically. If you want to know what your client is trying to say to you, sit back and receive his thoughts without verbal confusion. If you would like a certain person to call you, send him the message. You cannot interfere with anyone's decision making process, but you can send your impressions and allow him to respond.

Telepathy is a great source of comfort and help for people who are vocally debilitated due to a stroke, laryngitis, paralysis, or coma. It can help them keep their mental and communicative processes working to aid them in recovery. *Telepathy* is a working ability for achieving a closer harmony with loved ones, especially when defenses and semantics separate you from them. By communicating telepathically, you can eliminate excess verbiage and reach a basic essence of communication.

When traveling in a foreign country where language is a barrier, ideas can be communicated telepathically by using mental pictures rather than words. *Telepathy* is a way of communicating with pets, plants, children, and other people whose language skills are limited or nonexistent. *Telepathy* can even be used to remind your wife or husband to pick up your clothes at the cleaners on the way home from work or to get the waiter's attention for you to pay the dinner bill before the movie you want to attend begins.

Telepathy is not just a talent used for demonstrations at parties or for audience tricks on television talk shows. It is a useful psychic ability to help you communicate more clearly with the people and physical life around you.

Questions and Answers

What do I do when I am unable to send messages to people but I can receive them?

You may not have met a *sender* who can send impressions strongly enough for you to receive them telepathically. Practice sending and receiving thoughts or messages with different people to experience your talents fully. If you find that you still can only receive thoughts telepathically, rather than send them, use your receiving ability to help you. It will give you a sense of discussions you are involved in and help you to increase your sensitivity to yourself and others. By working with your telepathic receiving ability, you also will be able to understand and work through any barriers you may have constructed that prevent a free flow of communication for you.

Is there a physical limit to the number of thoughts or impressions you can communicate?

Communication, telepathically or verbally, depends on the people involved with the communication. If you are tired, confused, lack focus or are involved with mental or emotional problems you can limit the amount of communication. When you are balanced and open there is no limit to the amount of telepathic communication you can share with another person. Feelings, words, thoughts, sentences, or fragments of sentences can be transmitted and received frequently on a daily basis.

How can I protect my thoughts from being read by another person when I do not want to transmit them?

If you find yourself in a situation where you do not want to transmit your thoughts telepathically, clear your mind and focus on other thoughts or fill your mind with many thoughts so that you do not give focus to the thoughts you do not wish to send. Use your body communication to help you refocus and block any thoughts from being transmitted.

If I send a mental picture and then focus on a word to describe the picture will it interfere with what I wish to communicate?

As long as the word describes the object you are focusing on, the *receiver* still will gain the essence of what you are communicating. When you are beginning to explore your telepathic ability, try to focus on one image or word so that you do not confuse yourself and thus confuse the *receiver*. In this way your energy will flow directly to the *receiver* without any interference from you. If you find yourself losing focus or becoming distracted during the communication, trust your *gut response* and use a close variation of the message to be sent. Try to be as consistent as possible when you are sending a message so that the communication will be advantageous to you both.

If I am both a sender *and a* receiver, *which part of my ability should I focus on using?*

Being both a *sender* and a *receiver* gives you a choice of possibilities when communicating telepathically. Depending on your comfort or the nature of the situation, you can choose easily which way you can use your ability to aid in the communication. Because you are both a *sender* and *receiver*, your telepathic conversation can be more flexible, especially when another person who is a *sender* and *receiver* is involved.

sixteen

PSYCHIC CHILDREN

Remember when *imaginary playmates* spoke with you like trusted friends? When the scruffiest alley cat only came to you for feeding? When you woke from a dream and believed it really could happen? When your mother touched your fevered brow and you felt well again?

All of us were psychic children. Some of us are still. As children, we sensed everything, because we had no words through which to sort to describe what we encountered. Dolls and puppets and outlaws were as real to us as the people in our families. As psychic children, we shared ourselves openly, in an intangible way that was comforting and safe, in a world that drew no boundaries and where loving was a way of living.

Children still lie within us. They are the most physical representation of ourselves when we are in harmony with each other and our universe. Physical living sometimes shadows our inner children causing us to quickly devise armor and disguises to camouflage them. We become conditioned to look at others as being devoid of the natural honesty and willingness we experienced as children.

Psychic children sense the energy around them. Often, they react to it. They may become withdrawn, finding physical and emotional defenses to protect themselves. They may be hyperactive, unable to understand emotionally and mentally the defenses and conditioning of those around them who were once *psychic children* themselves. They are sensitive children, quiet children, children who speak out when they perceive things, and children who hold within themselves their basis talents, too afraid to express them in a world of armor and defenses. When they do react to inequities, they are disregarded, scolded, or repressed by adults who, as psychic children, also were taught to forego their natural abilities and trust those adult voices that were the loudest and most authoritarian.

When their parents house ill feelings toward one another, they sense these energies. When their teachers are upset, they experience this frustration and call it their own. When their baby sitters are annoyed, they are distressed and feel it is their fault. Having known their physical bodies for a short time, they are not yet equipped to rely on them. They only react. They are then told to be quiet, to go to their rooms, or to stop acting stupidly. Years of these life patterns pull them away from their natural impulses and they become, like the adults before them, confused, frustrated, and unhappy.

When a child talks about *spirit* friends, dream memories, or their natural ideas, they are not taken seriously or are ignored. Slowly they retreat from themselves, only to try, at some later date, to return to the nature of their being. A person, no matter how small or young, has his own wisdom and capabilities. His physical years of experiencing and growing are just beginning. His nonphysical energy has always been.

When is the last time you listened to a child? As parents or friends of children, you can help them to maintain their own special beauty and add to it. By valuing them as human beings, you can allow them to trust themselves and share and learn from your physical knowledge. By respecting them you will help them to respect themselves and others without losing themselves to defenses and deterrents. They will love themselves and love you so that you both can share and grow together. Whether old or young, large or small, we are all teachers and students. A wealth of knowing can be shared with children, teaching us how to remain whole, both physically and nonphysically, as we grow.

If you are a parent or have a child friend, look at them for a moment. Do they remind you of yourself? Do you allow them to voice their opinions, or do you control their insights, refuse their wisdom and repress their desires? As children, they bring with them their own abilities, both psychic and creative, to help them better their lives. By directing them rather than controlling, disciplining them rather than repressing, and guiding them rather than preaching, you can also, with their aid, develop those aspects of yourself.

By reinforcing their efforts to be who they are, rather than whom you would like them to be or whom you would like to be, you allow them the freedom to explore and assume their own self responsibility.

Psychic children bring to us the benefit of equal loving without prerequisites. They are open about their problems and threatening to adults who do not feel complete inside themselves. If you live with or know a child who is reactive to stimulation, hypersensitive or hyperactive, rather than reject them, open yourself to them and help them to learn about themselves. They have much to offer and much to learn. If your child voices a perception that is right, support him. If your child is wrong, explain the reason why.

Children are not adults. They are unsure of the mental and emotional ways of the body. They are unused to achieving their physical potential. Adults can help them. Children, in turn, can aid adults in returning to the children inside themselves and tapping their creative and nonphysical potential. If you can be honest with yourself, a child can help guide you away from smothering defenses that hinder you, and you can help them to see and enjoy themselves more fully.

If your basis for equality is loving, rather than experience, both you and the child can share. If you do not want the child to have that extra cookie, do not tell him there are no cookies left. Psychically he will know the reality of the situation. By being honest, you will prompt him to continue to be honest in his dealings with other people. You are not responsible for the development of any child. They are people unto themselves. They, like you, already have their abilities, talents, and resources inside themselves to draw upon. You, like them, can share and grow on the many levels of being. There is no race to be the best parent or friend to a child. Accept them and help them with their growing and they will help you in the best way they know, by being themselves.

There are many exercises to share with children you love. Any of the following exercises can be mutually experienced as ways to develop talents and grow together.

Exercises: For Psychic Children

Before using any exercise, share your knowledge of *preliminaries*, body channels, and body and *spirit* communication. These steps will not harm any child. In fact, children use them easily. A child, still in touch with his or her psychic abilities, will use natural barometers when deciding which exercise or *preliminary* step is most useful. Release your control and defenses and allow the children to explore their beauty, to apply it in their daily lives.

Psychic Reading

Teach your child to trust his *gut response* and to verbalize his perceptions about people and things he encounters.

Have your child go through his day reading people, sensing his own *gut response* to conversations and situations, and then verbalizing them to you. Have him sense other people and then follow through, in actions, what he is sensing. For example, if a parent is tired, instead of reacting to this lack of interest, let your child read the parent and act according to the information he is receiving. Rather than feeling rejected, the child will see the parent as a human being and will respect his feelings and try to comfort him.

If the child has siblings or friends, have him read them as they interact, so that a true understanding of the other person is evident to him. When he listens to your conversations with your friends, allow him to verbalize later his impressions of the people and what they are saying. In time he will begin to learn to determine what his *gut response* is and what he is thinking. He will learn, through practice, that these perceptions are not judgmental and can help him to communicate needs and desires more easily with those around him.

Take him with you when you go shopping, to the office, or to social functions. Let him observe co-workers, customers, cashiers, and acquaintances and verbalize his impressions of them. You will find that his perceptions may be insightful and in agreement with your own.

Psychometry

When shopping in the supermarket or department store, let your child hold in his hands, one at a time, the two toys he desperately wants to sense which one is better for him.

Take him to the library or bookstore and let him choose his reading matter, not by looking at the pretty cover, but by holding each book in his hand and sensing it. When a book is chosen, let him hold the book and verbalize his impressions of the story. Then read the story together to see how accurate he was.

Open the family album and show him pictures of his relatives, either known or unknown to him, and allow him to read their photographs. Validate any information with your own knowledge of these people. You will find that the next time a relative he has read comes to visit, he will see this person in depth rather than as one of an endless line of adults who have no relation to him or his life.

Auras

If your child wants a certain brand of cereal at the supermarket or is impatient with you while you are shopping, include him when selecting items to buy. Let him read and compare the *auras* of products chosen to find the best one for your family. Children see *auras* easily, because it is a natural way of seeing things.

Show your child how to read *auras* of plants in the house or go for a walk and let him read the *auras* of the birds, leaves, trees, and people that pass by. If you go to a zoo, let your child read the aura of the animals you visit or let him read the *aura* of your family pet over a period of time to note changes in behavior.

By using his *aura reading* ability, he will understand and participate more fully in his physical environment. Plants no longer will be things that need to be watered sometimes, and animals will not be burdens to be fed and walked. By learning to read the *aura* of each, your child will appreciate and be more responsible for the care and nurturing of those living things around him.

Psychokinesis

Let your child practice lifting a friend using the *levitation* exercise or participate with grownups when moving a circular table. Set the horizontal on the television set to fluctuate and allow your child to try to change it. Give him an old key or spoon or watch that doesn't work and let him focus his energy on bending or fixing it.

Exploring *psychokinesis* will enable him to participate more physically with his environment and understand that things can be affected and changed without using force and brawn.

Telepathy

Let your child read your mind in the evening to discover when it is time for him to go to bed without having to ask you. Set a specific time inside your mind and allow him to receive it.

Think of a time when you want him to come home from playing with friends and communicate it to him telepathically.

Your child will learn to be more responsible and self disciplined without encouraging defenses in both of you.

When your child is away at camp or school or in a new situation, designate a mutual time when you will focus on each other. Through this, he will learn that your love and caring will always be there for him to touch upon when you are not physically present to comfort him.

Healing

Take two clay pots of the same size and fill them with equal amounts of the same soil. Plant eight seeds of a rapidly growing plant, like parsley or beans, in each container. Place both pots where they will receive same amounts of sunlight. Water each pot equally. Continue to maintain both plants.

Toss a coin to determine upon which pot your child will focus. Using both hands, have him place them around the pot to transmit healing energy to the chosen plant as in the *laying on of hands* exercise. Be sure he drains *excess energy* from both hands into an inanimate object before *laying on of hands*. Repeat *laying on of hands* two to three times daily while actively ignoring the other plant.

Chart the progress of both plants and note any differences in their growth.

Ask your child to place his hands upon you when you are not feeling well or allow you to do the same with him. By practicing *laying on of hands*, your child will become more responsive and able to reach out to those who are ill and to show his affection freely with knowing and caring.

Clairvoyance

Take an object and hide it in another room. When ready, return to the room where your child is waiting. Let him visualize the object and then find it. This exercise can be expanded to include the house, yard, or other physical areas available.

Take several marbles or candies of different colors and place them in a small box or envelope where they cannot be seen. If no box is available, you can enclose them inside your hand. Without showing your child, remove some of the objects from inside their cover. Let your child visualize the colors of the remaining objects and verbalize his impressions to you. Show him the results. This exercise can be expanded to include any other objects also selected.

Predictions

Place a bowl in a convenient area of your house. Let your child write down any predictions that come to him about members of the family, friends, himself, or the world around him. Place each prediction, with the date predicted, inside the bowl. After a reasonable time elapses or when a prediction comes true, find the written prediction and date it for accuracy.

This will enable your child to gain a better sense of people and events around him and their relationship to himself.

By using these exercises or variations of exercises included in each chapter, you will be able to share more closely in the development and growth of your child. You will find through experience that children are people unique unto themselves. There are no judgments or limits to this sharing except those that you create for yourself.

Questions and Answers

How can I help my child retain his or her impressions of guides without scaring him?

Terms are used for reference by grownups. If your child describes conversations, experiences, or communications with imaginary friends or people unknown to you, allow an open atmosphere between you for discussion. *Guides* are friends, and if your child perceives his or her *guide*, he will not be frightened. Fright begins when the child becomes so physically oriented that only those things touched or seen are valid. If the energy of a *guide* overwhelms a child, communicate with the *guide* so that it can help to alleviate this problem. A child will naturally desire to communicate with or ignore communication from a *guide*. If the child knows that you are open to his perceptions and fears, he will not hesitate to talk about them. His decision to recognize his *guides* or *imaginary playmates* is his own and should not be influenced either way by outside sources. This will encourage him to explore all options and friendships available to him.

Is there an age when a child's psychic abilities tend to fade?

Psychic abilities and their use depend on the person. Children are naturally comfortable using their psychic abilities throughout their daily life and when supported in doing so will incorporate them with their physical learnings. If repressed, a child will use his psychic abilities on a minimal level or in the privacy of his own experiences.

When children see monsters or things that frighten them, are they seeing spirits?

Children sometimes develop fears learned through their environment, the media, movies, books, and people close to them. At other times they react physically to the presence of confused or friendly *spirits* that are near to them. Children usually sense *spirits* as friends, *imaginary playmates* rather than monsters. The energies of these *spirits* are harmonious to their own energy.

If your child wakes fearfully from a dream or is afraid to go to sleep because of fear of monsters, talk to him about his fears. The fears may not be related to what he is perceiving but to a sense of loss of his own strength in dealing with such situations. If the fears persist, try to have your child sense other benign imaginary or nonphysical friends nearby and ask them to remain with him and protect him from this monster. He may in time ask his nonphysical friends to help him aid the monster so that it will not bother him again.

Will I be doing the right thing by helping my child develop his psychic abilities? Won't they possibly hurt him?

Your child already uses and has his psychic abilities within him. They are a natural part of each of us. Because they are natural, they will grow and develop with your child and will not overpower him.

If your child shows an interest in using one or more of his psychic abilities, it would benefit him if you help him understand his abilities and learn to use them positively, rather than try to deny or inhibit what are inherent parts of himself.

If my child has more ability than I do, isn't it wrong to rely on him for insights even when they are usually right?

Developing psychic ability is not a contest, nor it it a way of relieving yourself of your own responsibilities. By relying on your child's psychic ability, you may be denying your own psychic development. Each person has certain abilities to use and develop for his own learning. By relying on your child you are placing more responsibility on him to be correct and to assume your way of growing. You, in turn, become a judge and victim of another's perceptions. By relying on your own insights and sharing realizations individually received, you can share your loving and growing without burdens or restrictions to you or your child.

seventeen

BEGINNINGS

Imagine yourself living inside a beautiful house with many rooms designed to fill your every need. Doors and windows surround you. Beyond these openings are other houses, the sky, and beyond. You can rest comfortably within your house, and journey to enjoy the earth and sky, or visit others in their chosen houses. As often as you wish, you can venture outside your house to share dimensions of yourself and then return again.

Your body is that beautiful house. You live and breathe inside each room every day. Your house comforts, protects, and embraces you in all that you do. You can choose to close its doors, board its windows, and be alone. Without effort you can unlock each door and open every window to expose yourself to the wealth of your existence. The care and upkeep of your house reflects how comfortably you live inside it.

Within this book information and exercises have been offered to help you experience your house and explore the world beyond it more fully. There is no specific time for this experiencing. The capabilities and talents within you can open windows and doors that have been closed to you. There is no competition to perpetuate; no limit to their use. They will lead you through narrow corridors and expand them, disclose hidden rooms and brighten them; expose vistas of yourself and the world you have never seen and encourage you to use them. Your willingness to accept these talents and capabilities will help you appreciate the realm of your potential and enjoy your growth.

If you have spent most of your life waiting in darkness, seated inside your house before a gaping window, open yourself to this wonder. Step outside yourself, beyond the man-made structures, and rest within a natural setting. Among the trees, rocks, birds, flowers and the earth, you will begin to feel all that you are and can be. Breathe the air you share with nature. Watch the clouds merge and flow. Nature accepts change without right or wrong, always flowing and becoming. Every sound and voice penetrates your own. Each situation, person and living being you encounter touches you and teaches you, adding a part of its reflection to you.

Every moment sparks a pathway inside you to explore and extends to join with others tendering their own. These roads can be traveled without fear of sharing life as you go on. It is first, within your house, that you can find peace and recognize beauty. Without losing yourself you will find, emerging past shadows, that this peace and beauty will enliven and benefit the glow of the world.

INDEX